TAKE YOUR PET A
1001 Places to Stay W

by Heather MacLean V

second edition

M.C.E.
Chester, NJ

ISBN 0-9648913-0-1

Acknowledgements

The author wishes to acknowledge the efforts of David C. MacLean (Sr. & Jr) whose ideas and assistance were invaluable, Cynthia and Christa MacLean for their support, Karen Duncan Bonner whose artwork graces the cover, and Debbie Moro, Nicole Scott and Pam Morse for assistance with research, compilation, and production.

Most of all, I'd like to thank my patient husband Rob, without whose inspiration this would never have been possible. And, of course, my "Best Friend" Teddie.

Contents

Introduction

We adopted our beloved yellow lab, Teddie, from St. Hubert's
Giralda in Madison, New Jersey in 1993. Ever since then we have
wanted to be able to travel with him. During our first year with
Teddie, I set about excitedly planning trips to Cape Cod, Maine, and
Williamsburg (to name a few). It was then I discovered that many
places will not take pets as overnight guests.

At first I solicited every pet-loving friend, neighbor, and relative,
looking for pet-friendly accommodations. Fortunately someone had
recently taken their dog to Cape Cod and told me where to stay. All
was O.K. until we got stuck in a 3-hour traffic jam and I hadn't
guaranteed our reservations. Confident that this traffic jam would end
soon, we hesitated calling. (Big mistake - ALWAYS guarantee your
room, and call to double-check.) We never made it in time and our
room for four days was gone.

Still confident with my knowledge that there actually *were* hotels and
motels that took pets, we stopped at a gas station in the same town
and called all the closest proprietors. Nothing. I began to panic. We
called the surrounding several towns (all the hotels/motels). Nothing.
As we drove 20 miles back in the direction from which we came, I
vowed to put this guide together so that no one would ever have to go
through this trouble again.

TAKE YOUR PET ALONG is a guide to hotels, motels and other
establishments that welcome pets. This single guide covers all of the
lower 48 United States and Canada, and is arranged **regionally** to
help you locate accommodations near your chosen vacation site. It is
a user-friendly guide with easy-to-turn pages, designed to be kept in
your glove compartment for quick reference. So take it and your dog
or cat along and have a good time!!!

General Information

TAKE YOUR PET ALONG was designed with you and your pet in mind. It includes listings for individual establishments, as well as members of certain national chains that take pets.

Policies on pets in rooms vary from hotel to hotel. Some hotels in this guide have restrictions on the number of rooms in which pets are allowed. Others limit the size and number of pets allowed, or the handling of pets in the rooms and on hotel grounds.

To make your travelling as trouble-free as possible, and as a courtesy to the hotel, follow these simple guidelines when travelling with a pet.

1. **Always call ahead**. Confirm that the hotel takes pets, since changes in policies can occur on short notice. **Also note that clerks may not be fully aware of the pet policy**, so it's best to talk with the reservations desk or the manager on duty.

2. Explain that you're bringing a pet when you make your reservation. Provide details (number and size of pet(s), etc.) when requested.

3. Get the details on any hotel-specific pet policies, and make sure you can adhere to them. For example, if your dog barks incessantly when left alone, you may not be allowed to leave him unattended in a room.

4. Consider guaranteeing your reservation for late arrival, because travelling with pets adds a degree of unpredictability. If you end up not needing the room, remember to call and cancel; otherwise, you'll be charged for the room anyway.

5. Observe common-sense rules of pet etiquette, whether or not they are explicitly required by the hotel. A single bad experience with a pet can result in a change in hotel policy. Do your part to keep these establishments pet-friendly for future travelers.

A word of caution. While all the establishments in this guide accept pets (as of press time), circumstances do change, and (as pointed out above) not all hotels have the same policies. While this book will help you to locate pet-friendly accomodations, it's up to you to notify the hotel that you're bringing a pet and confirm any special srrsngements. Some simple advance planning will assure that your trip is successful for both you and your furry friend.

Major Hotels That Sometimes Allow Pets

The following national hotel chains accept pets at many locations, some of which are listed individually in this guide. Call the following toll-free numbers for other locations in which you're interested.

- Best Western   (800) 528-1234
- Budget Host   (800) 283-4678
- Budgetel   (800) 428-3438
- Clarion   (800) 228-2000
- Comfort   (800) 228-2000
- Compri   (800) 426-6774
- Days Inn   (800) 325-2525
- Doubletree   (800) 426-6774
- Downtowner   (800) 251-1962
- Econo Lodge   (800) 228-2000
- Embassy Suites   (800) 362-2779
- Fairmont Hotels   (800) 527-4727
- Friendship Inns   (800) 228-2000
- Hampton Inns   (800) 426-7866
- Hilton Hotels   (800) 445-8667
- Holiday Inns   (800) 465-4329
- Howard Johnson   (800) 654-2000
- L-K Inns   (800) 282-5711
- La Quinta Inns   (800) 531-5900
- Lexington   (800) 537-8483
- Loews   (800) 223-0888
- Master Host   (800) 251-1962
- Motel 6   (800) 466-8356
- Passport   (800) 251-1962
- Residence Inn   (800) 331-3131
- Scottish   (800) 251-1962
- Super 8   (800) 800-8000
- Vagabond Inns   (800) 522-1555
- Wandlyn Inns   (800) 561-0006
- Westin Hotels   (800) 228-3000
- Wyndham   (800) 822-4200

Major Chains That ALWAYS Accept Pets

We highly recommend that you patronize these friendly hotels with your well-behaved pets whenever you can. Please let them know that their policy of inclusion of your WHOLE family is the reason you will be loyal to them. And please be careful and good about caring for your pet whenever you visit so that the policies will never change.

• **Drury Inn**	(800) 325-8300	(Midwest)
• **Exel Inns**	(800) 356-8013	(TX/Midwest)
• **Four Seasons**	(800) 332-3442	(Throughout US)
• **Inns of America**	(800) 826-0778	(CA, FL, SC)
• **Red Roof Inns**	(800) 843-7663	(Eastern US)

Locations for each of these chains are provided in the following pages. Happy travels!

Forgot your pet's favorite food?

Here are the toll-free numbers of several pet food companies. They will tell you the nearest place to purchase your favorite product...OR they will ship it to you as soon as overnight!

• ProPlan/Provisions	(800) PROPLAN
• IAMS/Eukanuba	(800) 525-4267
• Nature's Recipe	(800) 843-4008
• Nutro Company	(800) 833-5330
• Hills/Science Diet	(800) 445-5777
• FROMM	(800) 325-6331
• Triumph/Hi-Tor	(800) 331-5144

<u>Drury Inn Locations</u> (Call 800-378-7946)

Alabama:	Mobile	
Arkansas:	Blytheville	
Colorado:	Colorado Springs	Denver
Georgia:	Atlanta (4)	
Illinois:	Champaign	Collinsville
	Fairview Heights	Marion
	Mt. Vernon	Schaumberg
	Springfield	
Indiana:	Evansville	Indianapolis
	Terre Haute	
Kansas:	Merriam	Overland Park
Kentucky:	Bowling Green	Paducah
Michigan:	Detroit	Frankenmuth
Missouri:	Cape Girardeau	Columbia
	Jackson	Joplin
	Kansas City	Popular Bluff
	Rolla	St. Joseph
	St. Louis	Sikeston
	Springfield	
North Carolina:	Charlotte	
Tennessee:	Memphis	Nashville
Texas:	Austin	Corpus Christi
	Dallas	Houston

Exel Inns Locations (Call 800-367-3935)

Illinois:	Chicago (5) Rockford	Moline
Iowa:	Cedar Rapids Waterloo	Davenport
Michigan:	Grand Rapids	
Minnesota:	Minneapolis	St. Paul
South Dakota:	Sioux Falls	
Texas:	Austin	Denton
Wisconsin:	Appleton Green Bay Madison Wausau	Eau Claire La Crosse Milwaukee (3)

Inns of America Locations (Call 800-826-0778)

California:	Bakersfield (2) Fairfield Lost Hills Sacramento (2) San Diego (2)	Barstow Fresno (2) Madera San Jose Tulare
Florida:	Jacksonville (2) Orlando (3) Tampa	Lantana Palm Beach
Georgia:	Atlanta area (3)	
South Carolina:	Columbia	

Four Seasons Hotel Locations (North America)

Austin, TX	Four Seasons	(512) 478-4500
Beverly Hills, CA	Wilshire	(310) 275-5200
Boston, MA	Four Seasons	(617) 338-4400
Chicago, IL	Four Seasons	(312) 280-8800
Chicago, IL	Ritz-Carlton	(312) 266-1000
Dallas, TX	Four Seasons	(214) 717-0700
Houston, TX	Four Seasons	(713) 650-1300
Los Angeles, CA	Four Seasons	(310) 273-2222
Maui, HI	Four Seasons	(808) 874-8000
Mexico, DF	Four Seasons	(52-5)230-1818
Ontario, CAN	Minaki Lodge	(807) 224-4000
Nevis, W. Indies	Four Seasons	(809) 468-1111
New York, NY	Four Seasons	(212) 758-5700
New York, NY	The Pierre	(212) 838-8000
Newport Beach, CA	Four Seasons	(714) 759-0808
Palm Beach, FL	Four Seasons	(407) 582-2800
Philadelphia, PA	Four Seasons	(215) 963-1439
San Francisco, CA	Four Seasons	(415) 775-4700
Santa Barbara, CA	Four Seasons	(805) 969-2261
Seattle, WA	Four Seasons	(206) 621-1700
Toronto, Ontario	Four Seasons	(416) 964-0411
Toronto, Ontario	Inn on the Park	(416) 444-2561
Vancouver, CAN	Four Seasons	(604) 689-9333
Washington, DC	Four Seasons	(202) 342-0444

Red Roof Inn Locations (Call 800 - 843-7663)

Alabama:	Birmingham	Mobile (2)
Arizona:	Phoenix	Tucson
Arkansas:	Little Rock	
California:	Anaheim San Dimas Santa Ana	Ontario San Francisco Victorville
Connecticut:	Hartford New London	Milford
Delaware:	Wilmington	
Florida:	Jacksonville (2) Naples Pensacola Tampa (3)	Kissimmee Orlando Tallahassee W. Palm Beach
Georgia:	Atlanta (8)	
Illinois:	Champaign Joliet Rockford	Chicago (8) Peoria Springfield
Indiana:	Elkhart Indianapolis (3) Merrillville	Fort Wayne Lafayette Michigan City
Iowa:	Cedar Rapids	
Kansas:	Kansas City	
Kentucky:	Lexington (2)	Louisville (3)
Louisiana:	Baton Rouge Shreveport	Lafayette West Monroe

Red Roof Inn Locations (Call 800 - 843-7663)

Maryland:	Aberdeen	Baltimore (3)
	Columbia	Gaithersburg
	Lanham	Laurel
	Oxon Hill	
Massachusetts:	Boston (2)	West Springfield
	Woburn	
Michigan:	Ann Arbor	Benton Harbor
	Detroit (11)	Flint
	Grand Rapids	Kalamazoo (2)
	Lansing East	Lansing West
	Saginaw	
Minnesota:	Minneapolis (2)	St. Paul
Mississippi:	Jackson (2)	Tupelo
Missouri:	Columbia	Kansas City (2)
	St. Louis (5)	Springfield
New Hampshire:	Nashua	Salem
New Jersey:	Edison	Meadowlands
	Mount Laurel	Parsippany
	Princeton (2)	Tinton Falls
New York:	Albany	Binghamton
	Buffalo (3)	Rochester
	Syracuse	Utica
North Carolina:	Asheville	Chapel Hill
	Charlotte (3)	Durham (2)
	Greensboro (2)	Greenville
	Hickory	Raleigh
	Statesville	

Red Roof Inn Locations (Call 800 - 843-7663)

Ohio:
Akron (2)	Canton
Cincinnati (5)	Cleveland (5)
Columbus (8)	Dayton (3)
St. Clairsville	Toledo (3)

Pennsylvania:
Allentown	Danville
Erie	Harrisburg (2)
Philadelphia (3)	Pittsburgh (4)
Washington	Wilkes-Barre
York	

South Carolina:
Charleston	Columbia (2)
Florence	Greenville
Hilton Head	Myrtle Beach

Tennessee:
Chattanooga	Johnson City
Knoxville (2)	Memphis (3)
Nashville (3)	

Texas:
Austin	Corpus Christi
Dallas (6)	DeSoto
El Paso	Houston (5)
Laredo	Plano
San Antonio	

Virginia:
Alexandria	Chesapeake
Hampton	Manassas
Richmond (2)	Virginia Beach

West Virginia:
Charleston (3)	Fairmont
Huntington	Parkersburg

Wisconsin:
Madison	Milwaukee

Travel Tips for Pets

1.   Be sure your pet is travel-ready.

Some pets should not be taken on road trips. These include: pets that get very sick in the car; pets that are currently ill; pets that misbehave and are destructive; or pets that bark loudly or howl if they are left alone in a room.

2.   Be sure your trip is pet-compatible.

If you intend to always leave your pet in the hotel room or the car, maybe he'd be better off at home. Plan your trip so you are visiting places you can bring the pet along.

3.   Bring the pet's normal food.

Changing the diet (as well as the setting), no matter how well-intentioned, can give an animal distress. Bring some of your pet's favorite treats and toys as well. Remember, it's his vacation too!

4.   Always carry plenty of water.

This can't be emphasized enough. Pets normally should always have a full bowl of fresh water, but when there is a stressful change, they need it even more.

5.   Make stops in the trip to prevent an accident.

It is always wise to make several stops in a long trip to relax even when travelling *without* a pet. *With* a pet, it becomes imperative that you make frequent stops so that the animal can relieve itself and get some needed exercise. Remember if a pet has an accident, it is not the fault of the pet but the owners' mistake. It is the responsibility of the owner to see that the pet is let out or walked a sufficient number of times, that the pet is not upset or nervous, and that there are no medical problems.

Never hit or verbally abuse a pet that has an accident; take the responsibility upon yourself and explain the situation to the pet in a quiet but firm tone.

6.   Keep your pet leashed.

Never let your pet off leash in an unfamiliar area. This is especially important at highway rest areas - too many tragedies have occurred at rest stops with unleashed animals.

7.   Try not to leave your pet in the car.

Every summer dogs (and small children!) die or are severely injured by being left unattended in enclosed vehicles. If you must leave a pet in a car for a short time, park in a shady area, leave the windows at least partially open, and provide water. Dogs have much less tolerance for heat than humans do.

In wintry weather, consider that some dogs enjoy a little cold (none enjoy bitter weather) and other dogs cannot tolerate it. A dog will show and tell you what it cannot tolerate; you just need to be sensitive to the communication.

Using This Book

This guide is divided by region. Within each region, states and provinces are arranged alphabetically, with towns arranged alphabetically under the respective state/province. Addresses and phone numbers are provided to assist you in making reservations.

Each entry in the guide also lists codes for amenities and cost, as described below. For ease of reference, the codess are also listed at the beginning of each geographical section.

Amenities

The amenities in this guide are the ones about which inquiries are most often made. Some hotels may have other advantages or facilities which are not listed here. It is adviseable to call ahead to find out what facilities are currently available. The amenities in this guide are broken down into the following letter codes:

Hotel Amenity Codes

A	Airport nearby
H	Handicapped access
HS	Hair salon on premises
G	Golf within 10 miles
NS	Non-smoking rooms available
OB	Facility is on the beach
P	Playground on premises
R	Restaurant on premises
S	Swimming on premises
SA	Sauna on premises
SK	Skiing within 25 miles
T	Tennis within 10 miles
N/A	Not available at press time

Costs

Prices for rooms are grouped into four categories, representing typical
rates for an average one night stay. Rates may vary by room type or
season. Call ahead to confirm actual room rates. Cost codes used in
this book are as follows.

Hotel Cost Codes

*	$30-60/night
**	$61-100/night
***	$101-150/night
****	$151 and up/night
W	Hotel has weekly rates only
N/A	Not available at press time

Note: costs may vary by season.

NORTHEAST

NORTHEAST

NORTHEAST

Connecticut
Maine
Massachusetts
Massachusetts - Cape Cod
New Hampshire
New York
Rhode Island
Vermont

Hotel Cost Codes (for average one-night stay)

*	$30-60/night
**	$61-100/night
***	$101-150/night
****	$151 and up/night
W	Hotel has weekly rates only

Note: costs may vary by season.

Hotel Amenity Codes

A	Airport nearby
H	Handicapped access
HS	Hair salon on premises
G	Golf within 10 miles
NS	Non-smoking rooms available
OB	Facility is on the beach
P	Playground on premises
R	Restaurant on premises
S	Swimming on premises
SA	Sauna on premises
SK	Skiing within 25 miles
T	Tennis within 10 miles

CONNECTICUT

LOCATION	AMENITIES	COST
Danbury Ramada Inn I-84 at Exit 8 Danbury, CT 06810 (203) 792-3800	H,R,S,T,NS	*
Cromwell Comfort Inn 111 Berlin Rd. Cromwell, CT 06416 (860) 635-4100	G,H,R,T	**
East Hartford Econo Lodge 927 Main St. E. Hartford, CT 06108 (860) 289-7781	R	*
Ramada East 100 E River Drive East Hartford, CT 06108 (860) 528-9703	H,R,S,T,NS,SA	*
East Windsor Best Western Colonial 161 Bridge Street East Windsor, CT 06088 (860) 623-9411	A,G,S,NS	*
Farmington The Centennial 5 Spring Lane Farmington, CT 06032 (860) 677-4647	R,S,G	**

Hartford
Ramada Inn Cap. Hill 1   H,R,NS   *
440 Asylum St
Hartford, CT 06103
(203) 246-6591

Econo Lodge   R   **
927 Main St.
Hartford, CT 06108
(203) 289-7781

Litchfield
Toll Gate Hill   R,SK   ***
Route 202, P.O. Box 1339
Litchfield, CT 06759
(203) 567-4545

Manchester
Clarion Suites Inn   G,H,R,SK   ***
191 Spencer St.
Manchester, CT 06040
(203) 643-5811

Meriden
Ramada Inn   H,R,S,T,NS,SA   *
275 Research Parkway
Meriden, CT 06450
(203) 238-2380

Milford
Comfort Inn   G,H,R,SA   **
278 Old Gate Ln.
Milford, CT 06460
(203) 877-9411

Mystic
Howard Johnson Lodge   R   **
Exit 90 off I-95
Mystic, CT
(203) 536-2654

New Britain
Ramada Inn 3   G,H,R,NS   *
65 Columbus Blvd
New Britain, CT 06051
(860) 224-9161

New Haven
Howard Johnson Hotel   A,R,S,NS   **
400 Sargent Drive
New Haven, CT 06511
(203) 562-1111

Quality Inn   G,R,S,SA   **
100 Pond Lily Ave.
New Haven, CT 06525
(203) 387-6651

New London
Oakdell Motel   R   **
983 Hartford Rd.
New London, CT
(203) 442-9446

Red Roof Inn   R   **
707 Coleman St.
New London, CT
(203) 444-0001

Plainville
Howard Johnson Lodge   H,R,S,NS   *
400 New Britain Avenue
Plainville, CT 06062
(860) 747-6876

Riverside
Howard Johnson Lodge   R,S,NS   *
1114 Boston Post Road
Riverside, CT 06878
(203) 637-3691

Simsbury
The Simsbury 1820 House   R   **
731 Hopmeadow Street
Simsbury, CT 06070
(203) 658-7658

Vernon
Howard Johnson Lodge   H,R,S,NS   *
451 Hartford Turnpike
Vernon, CT 06066
(860) 875-0781

Waterbury
Red Bull Inn   G,H,R,S,T,NS,SK   *
300 Schraffts Drive
Waterbury, CT 06705
(203) 597-8000

Wethersfield
Ramada Inn Wethersfield 4   A,G,H,S,T,NS,SK   *
I-91 Exit 24 on Rt 99
Wethersfield, CT 06109
(203) 563-2311

MAINE

Auburn
Quality Inn   H,R,SK   **
1777 Washington St.
Auburn, ME 04210
(207) 783-1454

Bangor
Comfort Inn   G,H,R,T   *
750 Hogan Rd.
Bangor, ME 04401
(207) 942-7899

Rodeway Inn 482 Odlin Rd. Bangor, ME 04401 (207) 942-6301	G,R,T	*
Ramada Inn 357 Odlin Road Bangor, ME 04401 (207) 947-6961	A,G,H,R,S,NS	**

Bar Harbor

Quality Inn SR 3 & Mt. Desert St. Bar Harbor, ME 04609 (207) 288-5403	G,H,R,T	**
Days Inn SR 3 Bar Harbor, ME 04609 (207) 288-3321, (800) 325-2525	G,H,T	**
Balance Rock Inn 21 Albert Meadow Bar Harbor, ME 04609 (207) 288-9900	R,S	***
Bar Harbor Inn Newport Drive, P.O. Box 7 Bar Harbor, ME 04609 (207) 288-3351	R,S	***
Wonderview Inn SR 3 Bar Harbor, ME 04609 (207) 288-3358	R,S	***

Additional Bar Harbor Lodging:

Kelley's Cottages	(207) 288-3129
Rose Eden Cottages	(207) 288-3038
Hanscom's Motel	(207) 288-3744
Ocean Drive Motor Ct.	(207) 288-3361
The Ryan Estate	(207) 288-5154

NORTHEAST

Ellsworth
Comfort Inn   H,R   *
130 High St.
Ellsworth, ME 04605
(207) 667-1345

Freeport
Freeport Inn   R   ***
335 US 1 South
Freeport, ME 04032
(207) 865-3106

Isaac Randall House   R   ***
5 Independence Drive
Freeport, ME 04032
(207) 865-9295

Kittery
Kittery Motor Inn   R,S   **
Rt. 1 Bypass
Kittery, ME 03904
(207) 439-2000

Enchanted Nights   R   ***
29 Wentworth St.
Kittery, ME 03904
(207) 439-1489

Portland
Howard Johnson Hotel   A,R,S,NS   *
155 Riverside
Portland, ME 04103
(207) 774-5861

South Portland
Howard Johnson Hotel   A,H,R,S,NS   **
675 Main Street
South Portland, ME 04106
(207) 775-5343

NORTHEAST

Best Western   G,H,NS,S   **
700 Main St.
South Portland, ME 04106
(207) 774-6151

Sheraton Tara Hotel   G,H,R,NS,S,T   ***
363 Maine Mall Rd.
South Portland, ME 04106
(207) 775-6161

Waterville
Econo Lodge   G,R,T,SK   *
455 Kennedy Memorial Dr.
Waterville, ME 04901
(207) 872-5577

Best Western Waterville   R,S,NS   *
356 Main Street
Waterville, ME 04901
(207) 873-3335

MASSACHUSETTS

Boston
The Four Seasons   R   ****
200 Boylston St.
Boston, MA 02116
(617) 338-4400

Ritz Carlton   R   ****
15 Arlington St.
Boston, MA 02117
(617) 536-5700

Boston Harbor Hotel   R   ****
70 Rowes Wharf
Boston, MA 02110
(800) 752-7077

NORTHEAST

Howard Johnson Hotel   A,R,S,NS   **
200 Stuart Street
Boston, MA 02116
(617) 482-1800

Howard Johnson Hotel   A,R,S,NS   *
575 Commonwwealth Ave
Boston, MA 02215
(617) 267-3100

Howard Johnson Lodge   A,R,S,NS   **
1271 Boylston Street
Boston, MA 02215
(617) 267-8300

Cambridge
Howard Johnson Hotel   R,S,NS   **
777 Memorial Drive
Cambridge, MA 02139
(617) 492-7777

The Charles Hotel   R,S   ***
One Bennett at Eliot St.
Cambridge, MA 02138
(800) 882-1818

Chelmsford
Best Western   H,S,NS   *
187 Chelmsford Street
Chelmsford, MA 01824
(508) 256-7511

Concord
The Colonial Inn   R   ***
48 Monument Square
Concord, MA 01742
(800) 370-9200

Best Western   H,R,S,NS   **
Route 2 & Elm Street
Concord, MA 01742
(508) 369-6100

NORTHEAST

Danvers
Marriott Residence Inn   N/A   ***
51 Newbury St.
Danvers, MA 01923
(508) 777-7171

Falmouth
Quality Inn   G,R,S,SA   *
291 Jones Rd.
Falmouth, MA 02540
(508) 540-2000

Hadley
Howard Johnson Lodge   H,R,S,NS   *
401 Russell Street
Hadley, MA 01035
(413) 586-0114

Kingston
The Inn at Plymouth Bay   R,S,NS   **
Route 3 or 3A, 149 Main Street
Kingston, MA 02364
(617) 585-3831

Lexington
Battle Green Inn   N/A   **
1720 Massachusetts Ave.
Lexington, MA 02173
(617) 862-6100

Marlborough
Best Western Royal Plaza   R   ***
181 Boston Post Rd.
Marlborough, MA 01752
(508) 460-0700

Super 8   R   **
880 Donald J. Lynch Blvd.
Marlborough, MA 01752
(508) 460-1000

NORTHEAST

Revere
Howard Johnson Lodge   A,R,NS   **
407 Squire Road
Revere, MA 02151
(617) 284-7200

Salem
The Salem Inn   R   ***
7 Summer Street
Salem, MA 01970
(508) 741-0680

The Stephen Daniels House   R   **
1 Daniels St.
Salem, MA 01970
(508) 744-5709

Somerset
Quality Inn   H,R,S   *
1878 Wilbur Ave.
Somerset, MA 02725
(508) 678-4545

Springfield
Friendship Inn   G,R   *
1356 Boston Rd.
Springfield, MA 01119
(413) 783-2111

Sturbridge
The Publick House Motor Lodge R,G   **
Route 131
Sturbridge, MA 01566-0187
(800) PUBLICK

Econo Lodge   G,H,R,T   *
682 Main St.
Sturbridge, MA 01518
(508) 347-2324

Tewksbury
Marriott Residence Inn   R   ***
1775 Andover St.
Tewksbury, MA 01876
(508) 640-1003

Westborough
Comfort Inn Westborough   A,G,H,R,NS,SK   *
399 Boston-Wor.Tnpke (Rt. 9)
Westborough, MA 01581
(508) 366-0202

Marriott Residence Inn   R   ***
25 Connector Rd.
Westborough, MA 01581
(508) 366-7700

West Springfield
Econo Lodge   G,R,SK   **
1533 Elm St.
West Springfield, MA 01089
(413) 734-8278

Woburn
Ramada Hotel Woburn 2   G,H,R,S,NS   *
15 Middlesex Canal Park Road
Woburn, MA 01801
(617) 935-8760

Worchester
Econo Lodge   G,H,R,SK   *
531 Lincoln St.
Worchester, MA 01605
(413) 852-5800

MASSACHUSETTS - CAPE COD

Bass River
Wayfarers All Cottages   OB   W
186 Seaview Ave.
P.O. Box 123
Bass River, MA 02664
(508) 771-4532

Brewster
Chapins Bed & Breakfast   OB   W
216 Sheep Pond Dr.
Brewster, MA 02631
(508) 896-8210

High Brewster Inn   R   *
964 Satucket Rd.
Brewster, MA 02631
(508) 896-3636

Buzzards Bay
Bay Motor Inn   R,T,OB,G,P   *
223 Main St.
Buzzards Bay, MA 02532
(508) 759-3989

Centerville
Corners Motor Lodge   P,S,G,T,SA   W
Craigville Beach
Centerville, MA 02632
(800) 242-1137

Chatham
Morgan Cottages   OB   W
444 Old Harbor Rd.
Chatham, MA 02633
(508) 945-1870

Dennis Port

Captain's Row 257 Old Wharf Rd. Dennis Port, MA 02639 (508) 398-3117	N/A	W
Cricket Court 130 Route 28 Dennis Port, MA 02639 (508) 398-8400	G	W
Dolphin Cottages 291 Lower County Rd. Dennis Port, MA 02639 (508) 398-1551	N/A	W
Lamplighter Motor Lodge 329 Main St. Dennis Port, MA 02670 (508) 398-8469	G,P,S,T	W
Marine Lodge Cottages North St. Dennis Port, MA 02639 (508) 398-2963	P,T	W
Sea Lord Resort Motel 56 Chase Ave. Dennis Port, MA 02670 (508) 398-6900	G,OB	W
Town Cottages 319 Main St. Dennis Port, MA 02639 (508) 398-8469	G,P,S	W

Eastham

Gibson Cottages Long Pond Eastham, MA 02642 (508) 255-0882	OB	W

NORTHEAST

Town Crier Motel Rte. 6 Eastham, MA 02642 (800) 932-1434	R,S	**

East Sandwich

Azariah Snow House Rte. 6A East Sandwich, MA 02537 (508) 888-6677	OB	W
Earl of Sandwich Manor Motel 378 Rte. 6A East Sandwich, MA 02537 (508) 888-1415	G,R	*
Pine Grove Cottages Rte. 6A East Sandwich, MA 02537 (508) 888-8179	G,P,R	W
Wingscorton Farm 11 Wing Blvd. East Sandwich, MA 02537 (508) 888-0534	OB	W

Falmouth

Mariner Motel 555 Main St., Route 28 Falmouth, MA 02540 (508) 548-1331	R,S	W
Quality Inn 291 Jones Rd. Falmouth, MA 02540 (508) 540-2000	R,S,SA	W

Harwich Port

Harbor Walk Guest House 6 Freeman St. Harwich Port, MA 02646 (508) 432-1675	G,T	*

Hyannis

Angel Motel Rte. 132 Hyannis, MA 02601 (508) 775-2440	S	*
Cascade Motor Lodge 201 Main St. Hyannis, MA 02601 (508) 775-9717	S	W
Embassy Lodging of Hyannis 98 High School Rd. Hyannis, MA 02601 (508) 775-6402	N/A	W
Glo-Min by The Sea 182 Sea St. Hyannis, MA 02601 (508) 775-1423	G,P,R,S	W
Harbor Village Marstons Ave, Box 635 Hyannis Port, MA 02647 (508) 775-7581	OB	W
Holiday Inn Rte. 132 Hyannis, MA 02601 (508) 775-6600	R,S,T	W
Hyannis Holiday Motel 131 Ocean St. Hyannis, MA 02601 (800) 423-1551	S	*
Hyannis Sands Motor Lodge 921 Rte. 132 Hyannis, MA 02601 (508) 790-1700	G,S,OB	W

NORTHEAST

Rainbow Resort Motel Rte. 132 Hyannis, MA 02601 (508) 362-3217	G,S,OB	*
Sea Breeze by The Beach 397 Sea St. Rear, Box 553 Hyannis Port, MA 02647 (508) 775-4269	N/A	W
Seacoast on the Towne 33 Ocean St. Hyannis, MA 02601	N/A	**

Nantucket

10 Hussey Street Nantucket, MA 02554 (508) 228-9552	N/A	***
The Grey Lady 34 Center Street Nantucket, MA 02554 (508) 228-9552	N/A	***
The Boat House 15 Old North Wharf Nantucket, MA 02554 (508) 228-9552	N/A	***

North Truro

Seascape Motor Inn Shore Rd. North Truro, MA 02652 (508) 487-1225	OB	*

Orleans

Orleans Holiday Motel Rte. 6A&28 Orleans, MA 02653 1-800-451-1833	G,R,S,T	**

Skaket Beach Motel Rte. 6A Orleans, MA 02653 (508) 255-1020	S,NS	**

Provincetown

Hargood House Apt. 493-A Commerical St. Provincetown, MA 02657 (508) 487-9133	OB	W
White Wind Inn 174 Commerical St. Provincetown, MA 02657 (508) 487-1526	OB	W
Breakwater Motel Rte. 6A Provincetown, MA 02657 (508) 487-1134	OB	W
Holiday Inn Rte. 6A Provincetown, MA 02657 (800) 422-4224	R	**
White Sands Motel Rte. 6A, Box 611 Provincetown, MA 02657 (508) 487-0244	S,OB,SA	W

Sandwich

Dillingham House 71 Main St. Sandwich, MA 02563 (508) 833-0065	R,OB	**
Sandwich Lodge 54 Rte. 6A Sandwich, MA 02563 (508) 888-2275	R,S	**

NORTHEAST

South Chatham
Pine Oaks Cottages   OB   W
314 Cockle Cove Rd.
South Chatham, MA 02659
(508) 432-0892

South Dennis
Captain Nickerson Inn   G   W
333 Main St.
South Dennis, MA 02660
(800) 282-1619

South Harwich
Handkerchief Shoals Motel   G,S,T   W
Rte. 28, Box 306
South Harwich, MA 02661
(508) 432-2200

South Orleans
Ridgewood Cottages   G,T   W
Rte. 28 & 39, Box 82
South Orleans, MA 02662
(508) 255-0473

Ridgewood Motel   G,T   **
Rte. 28 & 39, Box 82
South Orleans, MA 02662
(508) 255-0473

South Wellfleet
Drummer Boy Condominium   N/A   W
Cannon Hill Rd.
South Wellfleet, MA 02663
(508) 349-3514

South Yarmouth
Brentwood Cottages   S,SA   W
961 Main St.
South Yarmouth, MA 02664
(508) 398-8812

NORTHEAST

Brentwood Motor Inn Route 28 South Yarmouth, MA 02664 (508) 398-8812	S,SA	*
Brentwood Townhouses Rte. 28, 961 Main St. South Yarmouth, MA 02664 (508) 398-0299	S,SA	**

Wellfleet

Brown's Landing P.O. Box 1017 Wellfleet, MA 02667 (508) 548-4540	N/A	W
Friendship Cottages Chequessett Neck Rd. Wellfleet, MA 02667 (508) 349-3390	OB	W

West Dennis

Amherst Vacation Homes 25 Magnolia Rd. Melrose, MA 02176 (617) 665-6259	T,OB	W
Captain Varrieur's Cottages Box 1332 West Dennis, MA 02670 (508) 394-4338	N/A	W
Pine Cove Inn Rte. 28 & Main St. West Dennis, MA 02670 (508) 398-8511	G,OB	W
Woodbine Village on the Cove Rte. 28 West Dennis, MA 02670 (508) 881-1381	OB	W

NORTHEAST

Elmwood Inn   N/A   *
57 Old Main St.
West Dennis, MA 02670
(508) 394-2798

West Yarmouth
Windrift Vacation Resort   R,S   W
115 Rte. 28
West Yarmouth, MA 02673
(508) 775-4697

Yarmouth Shores   OB   W
29 Lewis Bay Blvd.
West Yarmouth, MA 02673
(508) 775-1944

Yarmouth Port
Fisher's Net   NS,R   *
626 Main St.
Yarmouth Port, MA 02675
(508) 362-8264

Village Inn   N/A   *
Main St.
Yarmouth Port, MA 02675
(508) 362-3182

NEW HAMPSHIRE

Concord
Econo Lodge   G,R,T,SK   *
Gulf St.
Concord, NH 03301
(603) 224-4011

Franconia
The Hilltop Inn   R,SK   **
Main St.
Franconia, NH 03585
(603) 823-5695

The Horse and Hound Inn   R,SK   **
205 Wells Rd.
Franconia, NH 03580
(603) 823-5501

Littleton
Eastgate Motor Inn   SK   **
RFD 1
Littleton, NH 03561
(603) 444-3971

Manchester
Econo Lodge   G,H,R   *
75 W. Hancock St.
Manchester, NH 03102
(603) 624-0111

Howard Johnson Hotel   A,R,S,NS   *
298 Queen City Avenue
Manchester, NH 03102
(603) 668-2600

Merrimack
Ramada Hotel   A,G,H,R,S,NS,SK   *
Exit 11, Everett Turnpike
Merrimack, NH 03054
(603) 424-6181

Marriott Residence Inn   R   **
246 Daniel Webster Hwy
Merrimack, NH 03054
(603) 424-8100

North Conway
Maple Leaf Motel   SK   **
Box 917, Route 16
North Conway, NH 03860
(603) 356-5388

NORTHEAST

Portsmouth
Howard Johnson Hotel   A,H,R,S,NS   *
Interstate Traffic Circle
Portsmouth, NH 03801
(603) 436-7600

NEW YORK

Albany
Econo Lodge   G,H,R   *
1632 Central Ave.
Albany, NY 12205
(518) 456-8811

Howard Johnson Lodge   H,R,S,NS   *
Route 9W, 416 S. Blvd
Albany, NY 12209
(518) 462-6555

Marriott Residence Inn   R, S   ***
1 Residence Inn Drive
Latham, NY 12110
(518) 783-0600

Armonk
Ramada Inn   A,H,R,S,NS   **
I-684 Exit 3 S.
Armonk, NY 10504
(914) 273-9090

Batavia
Friendship Inn   G,R,T   *
8212 Park Rd.
Batavia, NY 14020
(716) 343-2311

Binghamton
Comfort Inn   G,H,R,T,SK   *
1156 Front St.
Binghamton, NY 13905
(607) 722-5353

HoJo Inn   H,R,S,NS   *
690 Front Street, I-81
Binghamton, NY 13905
(607) 724-1341

Marriott Residence Inn   N/A   **
4610 Vestal Parkway
Vestal, NY 13850
(607) 770-8500

Ramada Inn   G,H,R,S,NS,SA   *
65 Front Street
Binghamton, NY 13905
(607) 724-2412

Brockport
Econo Lodge   G,H,R,T   *
6575 4th Section Rd.
Brockport, NY 14420
(716) 637-3157

Buffalo
Marriott Residence Inn   R,S   ***
100 Maple Rd.
Williamsville, NY 14221
(716) 632-6622

Canandaigua
Econo Lodge   G,H,R,T,SK   *
170 Eastern Blvd.
Canandaigua, NY 14424
(716) 394-9000

Clay
Rodeway Inn   G,R,SK   **
901 S. Bay Rd.
Clay, NY 13041
(315) 458-3510

Commack
Howard Johnson Lodge   H,R,S,NS   *
450 Moreland Road
Commack, NY 11725
(516) 864-8820

Corning
Econo Lodge   G,H,R   **
200 Robert Damn Dr.
Corning, NY 14870
(607) 962-4444

Cortland
Econo Lodge   G,H,R,T   *
3775 US 11
Cortland, NY 13045
(607) 753-7594

Dunkirk
Econo Lodge   R,SK   *
310 Lake Shore Dr.
Dunkirk, NY 14048
(716) 366-2200

Vineyard Motel   G,R,SK   *
Vineyard Dr.
Dunkirk, NY 14048
(716) 366-4400

Elizabeth
Clarion Hotel   G,H,R,S   **
901 Spring St.
Elizabeth, NY 07201
(908) 527-1600

Farmington
Economy Inn   G,R,T,SK   **
6037 SR 96
Farmington, NY 14425
(716) 924-2300

Fishkill
Marriott Residence Inn   R   ***
2481 Route 9
Fishkill, NY 12524
(914) 896-5210

Fleishmanns
River Run   R,G,NS,SK   **
"The Inn for Pet Lovers"
Main Street
Fleischmanns, NY 12430
(914) 254-4884

Fulton
Quality Inn   G,H,R,T,SK   **
930 S. First St.
Fulton, NY 13069
(315) 593-2444

Hamburg
HoJo Inn   H,S,NS   *
5245 Camp Road
Hamburg, NY 14075
(716) 648-2000

Hornwell
Comfort Inn   G,H,R,S,SK   **
1 Canisteo Sq.
Hornwell, NY 14843
(607) 324-4300

Horseheads
Howard Johnson Lodge   A,R,S   *
Routes 17, 14 & 328
Horseheads, NY 14845
(607) 739-5636

Ithaca
Econo Lodge   G,H,R,T,SK   **
Cayuga Mall
Ithaca, NY 14850
(607) 257-1400

NORTHEAST

Howard Johnson Lodge   A,H,S,NS   *
2300 North Triphammer Road
Ithaca, NY 14850
(607) 257-1212

Ramada Inn Airport   A,G,H,R,S,NS,SA,SK   *
2310 North Triphammer Road
Ithaca, NY 14850
(607) 257-3100

Collegetown Motor Lodge   G,T   ***
312 College Ave.
Ithaca, NY 14830
(607) 273-3542; (800) 745-3542

Jamestown
Comfort Inn   G,H,R,T   *
2800 N. Main St.
Jamestown, NY 14701
(716) 664-5920

Lake George
Econo Lodge   G,H,R,S,T   **
431 Canada St.
Lake George, NY 12845
(518) 668-2689

Lake Placid
Howard Johnson Resort Lodge   H,R,S,T,NS   *
90 Saranac Avenue
Lake Placid, NY 12946
(518) 523-9555

Quality Inn   G,R,SK   **
122 Main St.
Lake Placid, NY 12946
(518) 523-1818

The Stagecoach Inn   R,G,SK   **
370 Old Military Rd.
Lake Placid, NY 12946
(518) 523-9474

Ramada Inn   R,G,NS,S,SK   **
8-12 Saranac Lake
Lake Placid, NY 12946
(518) 523-2587

Latham
Comfort Inn   G,H,R   **
866 Albany-Shaker Rd.
Latham, NY 12110
(518) 783-1216

Howard Johnson Lodge   A,H,R,S,NS   *
611 Troy-Schenactady Road
Latham,NY 12110
(518) 785-5891

Malone
Econo Lodge   G,H,R,SK   *
227 W. Main St.
Malone, NY 12953
(518) 483-0500

Middletown
Howard Johnson Lodge   H,R,S,NS   **
551 Route 211 East
Middletown, NY 10940
(914) 342-5822

Newark
Quality Inn   G,R,SA,SK   *
125 N. Main St.
Newark, NY 14513
(315) 331-9500

Newburgh
Howard Johnson Lodge   A,R,S,T,NS   *
95 Route 17K
Newburgh, NY 12550
(914) 564-4000

NORTHEAST

New York

The Carlyle	R	***
35 E. 76th St. & Madison Ave.		
New York, NY 10021		
(212) 744-1600		

The Waldorf Astoria	R	****
301 Park Ave.		
New York, NY 10022		
(212) 355-3000		

The Pierre	R	****
2 East 61st St.		
New York, NY 10021		
(212) 838-8000		

North River

Garnet Hill Lodge	N/A	**
13th Lake Rd.		
North River, NY 12856		
(518) 251-2821		

Norwich

Howard Johnson Hotel	A,H,R,S,NS	*
75 North Broad Street		
Norwich, NY 13815		
(607) 334-2200		

Ogdensburg

Quality Inn	G,R	*
SR 37, RD 4		
Ogdensburg, NY 13669		
(315) 393-4550		

Pembroke

Econo Lodge	G,H,R,T	*
8493 SR 77 Pembroke		
Pembroke, NY 14036		
(716) 599-4681		

Plainview
Marriott Residence Inn   R,S,SA   *
9 Gerhard Rd.
Plainview, NY 11803
(516) 433-6200

Plattsburgh
Howard Johnson Lodge   A,H,R,S,NS   *
PO Box 1278, I-87 & Route 3
Plattsburgh, NY 12901
(518) 561-7750

Rochester
Comfort Inn   G,R   *
395 Buell Rd.
Rochester, NY 14624
(716) 436-4400

Comfort Inn   G,H,R,T   **
1501 W. Ridge Rd.
Rochester, NY 14615
(716) 621-5700

Econo Lodge   G,H,R,T   **
940 Jefferson Rd.
Rochester, NY 14623
(716) 427-2700

Marriott Residence Inn   S,SA   ***
1300 Jefferson Rd.
Rochester, NY 14623
(716) 272-8850

Wellesley Inn   N/A   **
797 E. Henrietta Rd.
Rochester, NY 14623
(716) 427-0130

NORTHEAST

Rock Hill
Howard Johnson Lodge   R,S,NS   *
PO Box 469, Rock Hill Drive
Rock Hill, NY 12775
(914) 796-3000

Saranac Lake
Comfort Inn   G,H,R,S,SK   **
148 Lake Flower Ave.
Saranac Lake, NY 12983
(518) 891-1970

Spring Valley
Econo Lodge   G,R,T,SK   **
SR 59 East
Spring Valley, NY 10977
(914) 623-3838

Saugerties
HoJo Inn   R,S,NS   *
2764 Route 32
Saugerties, NY 12477
(914) 246-9511

Syracuse
Marriott Residence Inn   R,S   ***
6420 Yorktown Circle
Syracuse, NY 13057
(315) 432-4488

Comfort Inn   G,H,R,T,SK   *
454 James St.
Syracuse, NY 13203
(315) 425-0015

Howard Johnson Lodge   R,S,NS   *
Thompson Road at Carrier Circle
Syracuse, NY 13206
(315) 437-2711

Vestal
HoJo Inn   R,S,NS   *
3601 Vestal Parkay East
Vestal, NY 13850
(607) 729-6181

Watertown
Econo Lodge   G,H,R,S,SK   *
1030 Arsenal St.
Watertown, NY 13601
(315) 782-5500

Quality Inn   G,H,R,T,SK   *
1190 Arsenal St.
Watertown, NY 13601
(315) 788-6800

White Plains
Marriott Residence Inn   N/A   ***
5 Barker Ave.
White Plains, NY 10601
(914) 761-7700

RHODE ISLAND

Middletown
Howard Johnson Lodge   R,S,NS   *
351 West Main Road
Middletown, RI 02842-6309
(401) 849-2000

Newport
John Banister House   G   **
56 Pelham St.
Newport, RI 02840
(401) 846-0050

Providence
Providence Marriott   R,T,S   ***
Charles & Orms St.
Providence, RI 02903
(401) 272-2400

Warwick
Comfort Inn   A,H,R   **
1940 Post Rd.
Warwick, RI 02886
(401) 732-0470

Motel 6   A,R,S,NS   *
20 Jefferson Boulevard
Warwick, RI 02888
(401) 467-9800

Holiday Inn   R,T,S   **
801 Greenwich Ave.
Warwick, RI 02886
(401) 732-6000; (800)-HOLIDAY

VERMONT

Barre
Budget Inn   R,S,NS   *
573 North Main Street
Barre, VT 05641
(802) 479-3333

Bennington
Ramada Inn   G,H,R,S,T,NS,SA,SK   *
Route 7 & Kocher Drive
Bennington, VT 05201
(802) 442-8145

Burlington
Rodeway Inn   G,H,R,T   *
1860 Shelburne Rd.
Burlington, VT 05401
(802) 862-0230

Howard Johnson Lodge   A,R,S,NS   *
1 Dorsel Street
Burlington, VT 05403
(802) 863-5541

Craftsbury
The Inn On the Common   R   **
Craftsbury, VT
(802) 586-9619

Montpelier
Econo Lodge   G,R,T,SK   *
101 Northfield St.
Montpelier, VT 05602
(802) 223-5258

Rutland
HoJo Inn   R,S,NS   *
US Hwy. 7, Sth Main St.
Rutland, VT 05701
(802) 775-4303

South Woodstock
Kedron Valley Inn   R   ***
Route 106
South Woodstock, VT 05071
(802) 457-1473

Springfield
Holiday Express   H,R,S,NS   *
818 Charlestown Road
Springfield, VT 05156
(802) 885-4516

St. Albans
Econo Lodge   G,H,R,T   *
287 S. Main St.
St. Albans, VT 05478
(802) 524-5956

NORTHEAST

Stowe
Topnotch Resort and Spa   G, SK   ***
Mountain Road
Stowe, VT 05672
(802) 253-8585

The Green Mountain Inn   R,SK   ***
Main Street, P.O.Box 60
Stowe, VT 05672
(802) 253-7301

MID-ATLANTIC

MID-ATLANTIC

Delaware
District of Columbia
Maryland
New Jersey
Pennsylvania
Virginia
West Virginia

Hotel Cost Codes (for average one-night stay)

*	$30-60/night
**	$61-100/night
***	$101-150/night
****	$151 and up/night
W	Hotel has weekly rates only

Note: costs may vary by season.

Hotel Amenity Codes

A	Airport nearby
H	Handicapped access
HS	Hair salon on premises
G	Golf within 10 miles
NS	Non-smoking rooms available
OB	Facility is on the beach
P	Playground on premises
R	Restaurant on premises
S	Swimming on premises
SA	Sauna on premises
SK	Skiing within 25 miles
T	Tennis within 10 miles

DELAWARE

New Castle
Days Inn   H,R   *
I-295 & SR 9
New Castle, DE 19720
(302) 654-5400

Rodeway Inn   G,R,T   *
111 S. Dupont Hwy.
New Castle, DE 19720
(302) 328-6246

Quality Inn   R,T   *
147 N. Dupont Hwy.
New Castle, DE 19720
(302) 328-6666

Newark
Marriott Residence Inn   G,S   **
240 Chapman Rd.
Newark, DE 19702
(302) 453-9200

Comfort Inn   G,H,R   *
1120 S. College Ave.
Newark, DE 19713
(302) 368-8715

Howard Johnson Lodge   H,R,S,NS   *
1119 South College Ave
Newark, DE 19713
(302) 368-8521

Seaford
Comfort Inn   H,R,S,SA   **
US 13 & Beaverdam Dr.
P.O. Box 1450
Seaford, DE 19973
(302) 629-8385

Wilmington
Brandywine Valley Inn   N/A   **
1807 Concord Pike
Wilmington, DE 19803
(302) 656-9436

DISTRICT OF COLUMBIA (and vicinity)

Alexandria, VA
Comfort Inn   H,R   *
5716 S. Van Dorn St.
Alexandria, VA 22310
(703) 922-9200

Comfort Inn   G,H,R   *
7212 Richmond Hwy.
Alexandria, VA 22306
(703) 765-9000

Econo Lodge   R   *
700 N. Washington St.
Alexandria, VA 22314
(703) 836-5100

Howard Johnson Hotel   A,R,S,NS   **
5821 Richmond Highway
Alexandria, VA 22303
(703) 329-1400

Ramada Hotel/Old Town 2   A,H,R,S,NS   ***
901 N Fairfax Street
Alexandria, VA 22314
(703) 683-6000

Baileys Crossroads, VA
Econo Lodge   R,T   **
5666 Columbia Pike
Baileys Crossroads, VA 22041
(703) 820-5600

Beltsville, MD
Ramada Inn Calverton 4   H,R,S,T,NS   *
4050 Powder Mill Rd
Beltsville, MD 20705
(301) 572-7100

Bowie, MD
Econo Lodge   G,H,R   **
US 301 & 50 at SR 3
Bowie, MD 20718
(301) 464-2200

Cheverly, MD
Howard Johnson Lodge   H,S,NS   *
5811 Annapolis Road
Cheverly, MD 20784
(301) 779-7700

Fair Oaks, VA
Marriott Residence Inn   N/A   ***
Fairfax County Pkwy and Fair Lakes Pkwy
Fair Oaks, VA 22033
(800) 331-3131 (Opening Fall 1997)

Falls Church, VA
Comfort Inn (WA)   A,G,S,NS   *
6111 Arlington Blvd
Falls Church, VA 22044
(703) 534-9100

Gaithersburg, MD
Comfort Inn   G,H,R   **
16216 Fredrick Rd.
Gaithersburg, MD 20877
(301) 330-0023

Econo Lodge   H,R,T   *
18715 N. Fredrick Ave.
Gaithersburg, MD 20879
(301) 963-3840

MID-ATLANTIC

Herndon, VA
Marriott Residence Inn   N/A   ***
315 Elden St.
Herndon, VA 22070
(703) 435-0044

Laurel, MD
Comfort Suites   G,H,R,T   **
14402 Laurel Pl.
Laurel, MD 20707
(301) 206-2600

Manassas, VA
Best Western   G,H,R,S,NS   *
Interstate 66 & Route 234
Manassas, VA 22110
(703) 361-8000

New Carrollton, MD
Ramada Hotel 11   G,R,S,NS   *
8500 Annapolis Road
New Carrollton, MD 20784-3014
(301) 459-6700

Silver Spring, MD
Econo Lodge   G,R,T   *
7990 Georgia Ave.
Silver Spring, MD 20910
(301) 565-3444

Washington, DC
Red Roof Inn   H,R,SA   **
500 H. St.
Washington, DC 20001
(202) 289-5959

HoJo Inn   R,S,NS   *
600 New York Avenue NE
Washington, DC 20002
(202) 546-9200

Loews L'Enfant Plaza   R   ***
480 L'Enfant Plaza SW
Washington, DC
(202) 484-1000

The Four Seasons   R   ***
2800 Pennsylvania Ave. NW
Washington, DC
(202) 342-0444

Woodbridge, VA
Econo Lodge   G,R   *
13317 Gordon Blvd.
Woodbridge, VA 22191
(703) 491-5196

Friendship Inn   G,R   *
13964 Jefferson Davis Hwy.
Woodbridge, VA 22191
(703) 494-4144

MARYLAND (See DC listings for Washington suburbs)

Aberdeen
Econo Lodge   R   *
820 W. Bel Air Ave.
Aberdeen, MD 21001
(410) 272-5500

Murlyn Inn   G,H,R,T   *
424 S. Philadelphia Blvd.
Aberdeen, MD 21001
(410) 272-3666

Howard Johnson Lodge   H,R,S,NS   *
793 West Bel Air Avenue
Aberdeen, MD 21001
(410) 272-6000

Annapolis
Loews Hotel   N/A   ***
126 West Street
Annapolis, MD 21401
(410) 263-7777

Marriott Residence Inn   S, R   ***
170 Admiral Cochrane Dr.
Annapolis, MD 21401
(410) 573-0300

Baltimore
Howard Johnson Hotel   H,R,S,NS   *
5701 Baltimore National Pike
Baltimore, MD 21228-1797
(410) 747-8900

Baltimore Marriott Inner Harbor   R,T   ***
Pratt & Eutaw St.
Baltimore, MD
(410) 962-0202; (800) 228-9290

Marriott Residence Inn   N/A   ***
10710 Beaver Dam Rd.
Hunt Valley, MD 21030
(410) 584-7370

Cambridge
Quality Inn   G,H,R   *
US 50 & Crusader Rd.
Cambridge, MD 21613
(410) 228-6900

Columbia
Marriott Residence Inn   S, R   ***
4910 Executive Park Drive
Columbia, MD 21045
(800) 331-3131 (Opening Spring 1997)

Easton
Econo Lodge G,R *
8175 Ocean Gateway
Easton, MD 21601
(410) 820-5555

Elkton
Econo Lodge G,H,R *
311 Belle Hill Rd.
Elkton, MD 21921
(410) 392-5010

Frederick
Comfort Inn H,R,SK *
420 Prospect Blvd.
Frederick, MD 21701
(301) 695-6200

Holiday Inn Express R,SK **
5579 Spectrum Drive
Frederick, MD 21701
(301) 695-2881

Frostburg
Comfort Inn G,H,R,SA *
SR 36 N. Frostburg Indust. Park
Frostburg, MD 21532
(301) 689-2050

Gaithersburg
Econo Lodge N/A **
18715 N. Frederick Ave.
Gaithersburg, MD
(301) 963-3840

Glen Burnie
Glen Burnie Holiday Inn R,T ***
6323 Richie Hwy.
Glen Burnie, MD
(410) 636-4300

Grasonville
Comfort Inn G,R,S,SA **
US 50/301, Rt. 2
Grasonville, MD 21638
(410) 827-6767

Rodeway Inn G,H,R **
107 Hissey Rd.
Grasonville, MD 21638
(410) 827-7272

Jessup
Comfort Inn H,R,SA **
US 1 & SR 32
8828 Baltimore-Washington Blvd.
Jessup, MD 20794
(410) 880-3133

La Plata
Deluxe Inn G,H,R,T *
US 301 & SR 6
La Plata, MD 20646
(301) 934-1400

Linthicum
Marriott Residence Inn S, R ***
Nursery & Winterson
Linthicum, MD 21090
(800) 331-3131 (Opening Fall 1997)

Ocean City
Best Western G,H,R,T *
6007 Coastal Hwy.
Ocean City, MD 21842
(410) 524-6100

HoJo Inn H,R,S,NS *
102 60th Street, Bay Front
Ocean City, MD 21842
(410) 524-5634

Pikesville
Comfort Inn G,H,R,T **
10 Wooded Way
Pikesville, MD 21208
(410) 484-7700

Princess Anne
Econo Lodge H,R *
US 13, 10936 Market Ln.
Princess Anne, MD 21853
(410) 651-9400

Pocomoke City
Quality Inn G,H,R,T *
825 Ocean Hwy.
Pocomoke City, MD 21851
(410) 957-1300

Salisbury
Econo Lodge G,H,R *
712 N. Salisbury Blvd.
Salisbury, MD 21801
(410) 749-7155

Towson
Ramada Inn Towson 4 H,R,S,T,NS *
8712 Loch Raven Blvd
Towson, MD 21286
(410) 823-8750

Waldorf
Econo Lodge H,R *
US 301, Acton Ln.
Waldorf, MD 20601
(301) 645-0022

HoJo Inn H,R,S,NS *
3125 Crain Highway
Waldorf, MD 20602
(301) 932-5090

MID-ATLANTIC

Westminster
Comfort Inn   G,H,R   *
451 WMC Dr.
Westminster, MD 21158
(410) 857-1900

NEW JERSEY

Atlantic City
Marriott Residence Inn   S, R   ***
900 Mays Landing
Somers Point, NJ 08244
(609) 927-6400

Blackwood
HoJo Inn   H,R,S,NS   *
832 North Black Horse Pike
Blackwood, NJ 08012
(609) 228-4040

Bordentown
Econo Lodge   G,H,R,T   **
US 130 & 260
Bordentown, NJ 08505
(609) 298-5000

Cape May
Marquis de Lafayette   OB   ***
501 Beach Drive
Cape May, NJ 08204
(800) 257-0432, (609) 884-3500

Cabin City Motel   N/A   **
756 Route 9
Cape May, NJ 08204
(609) 884-8551

Cherry Hill
Marriott Residence Inn   N/A   ***
1821 Old Cuthbert Rd.
Cherry Hill, NJ 08034
(609) 429-6111

Clifton
Howard Johnson Lodge   H,R,S,NS   *
680 Route 3 West
Clifton, NJ 07014
(201) 471-3800

East Hanover
Ramada Hotel   G,H,T,NS,SA   **
130 Route 10 West
East Hanover, NJ 07936
(201) 386-5622

Summerfield Suites   H,NS   ***
1 Ridgedale Ave.
Whippany, NJ 07936
(201) 605-1001

East Windsor
Ramada Inn   G,H,R,S,NS,SA   *
399 Monmouth St.
East Windsor, NJ 08520
(609) 448-7000

Hope
The Inn at Millrace Pond   N/A   ***
P.O. Box 359
Hope, NJ 07844
(908) 459-4884

Lawrenceville
Howard Johnson Lodge   H,R,S,NS   *
2995 Brunswick Pike
Lawrenceville, NJ 08648
(609) 896-1100

MID-ATLANTIC

Mahwah
Comfort Inn   G,H,R,T,SK   **
160 SR 17 S.
Mahwah, NJ 07430
(201) 512-0800

Middletown
Howard Johnson Lodge   R,S,NS   **
750 Highway 35 South
Middletown, NJ 07748
(908) 671-3400

Monmouth/Tinton Falls
Marriott Residence Inn   S, R   ***
90 Park Road
Tinton Falls, NJ 07724
(908) 389-8100

Mt. Holly
Howard Johnson Lodge   H,R,S,NS   *
Route 541 & NJ Tpke Exit 5
Mt. Holly, NJ 08060
(609) 267-6550

New Brunswick
Econo Lodge   G,R,T   **
26 US 1
New Brunswick, NJ 08901
(908) 828-8000

Newark
Ramada Hotel   A,G,S,NS   **
Route One South
Newark, NJ 07114
(201) 824-4000

North Plainfield
Howard Johnson Lodge   H,R,T,NS   *
US 22 West at West End Ave.
North Plainfield, NJ 07060
(908) 753-6500

MID-ATLANTIC

North Wildwood
Long Beach Lounge	S,OB	**
539 East 9th Ave.		
North Wildwood, NJ 08260		
(609) 522-1520		

New England Motel	N/A	**
106 West 11th Street		
North Wildwood, NJ 08260		
(609) 522-7250		

Woodbury Motel/Apts.	H,G,T	**
407 Surf Ave.		
North Wildwood, NJ 08260		
(609) 522-7315		

Paramus
Howard Johnson Lodge	R,S,NS	*
393 Route 17		
Paramus, NJ 07652		
(201) 265-4200		

Parsippany
HoJo Inn	H,R,NS	*
625 Route 46 East		
Parsippany, NJ 07054		
(201) 882-8600		

Days Inn	H,R,G,NS	***
3159 Rt. 46		
Parsippany, NJ 07054		
(201) 335-0200		

Penns Grove
Howard Johnson Lodge	H,R,S,NS	*
10 Howard Johnson Lane		
Route 295 & NJ Turnpike		
Penns Grove, NJ 08060		
(609) 299-3800		

MID-ATLANTIC

Phillipsburg
Philipsburg Inn   R,S,NS   *
US 22 & I-78, Exit 3
Phillipsburg, NJ 08865
(908) 454-6461

Princeton
Marriott Residence Inn   S, SA, R   ***
4225 Rt. 1 , P.O. Box 8388
Princeton, NJ 08543
(908) 329-9600

Ramsey
Howard Johnson Lodge   R,S,NS   *
1255 Route 17 South
Ramsey, NJ 07446
(201) 327-4500

Rockaway
Howard Johnson Lodge   H,R,S,NS   **
Green Pond Road
Rockaway, NJ 07866
(201) 625-1200

Somerset
Ramada Inn   H,R,S,NS,SA   *
Weston Canal Rd.
Somerset, NJ 08873
(908) 560-9880

South Plainfield
Comfort Inn   R   *
I-287 & Stelton Rd.
South Plainfield, NJ 07080
(908) 561-4488

Toms River
Howard Johnson Lodge   H,R,S,NS   **
Route 37 & Hooper Ave.
Toms River, NJ 08753
(908) 244-1000

MID-ATLANTIC

Vineland
Ramada Inn Vineland   G,H,S,T,NS   *
2216 West Landis Ave.
Vineland, NJ 08360
(609) 696-3800

Wayne
Howard Johnson Lodge   H,R,S,NS   *
1850 Route 23 & Ratzer Rd.
Wayne, NJ 07470
(201) 696-8050

Warren
Somerset Hills Hotel   N/A   ***
200 Liberty Corner Rd. (I-78 Exit 33)
Warren, NJ 07059
(908) 647-6700

PENNSYLVANIA

Altoona
Econo Lodge   G,R,SK   *
2960 Pleasant Valley Blvd.
Altoona, PA 16601
(814) 944-3555

HoJo Inn   H,R,S,NS   *
1500 Sterling St.
Altoona, PA 16602
(814) 946-7601

Ramada Hotel   G,H,R,S,NS,SK   **
Rte. 220 Plank Road Exit
Altoona, PA 16601
(814) 946-1631

Bartonsville
Comfort Inn   H,R,SK   **
SR 611
Bartonsville, PA 18321
(717) 476-1500

MID-ATLANTIC

Holiday Inn   G,T,SK   **
Bartonsville, PA
(800) 231-3321

Rimrock Cottages   G,T,SK   **
Bartonsville, PA
(717) 629-2360

Bedford
Econo Lodge   G,R,T,SK   *
RD 2, Transport St.
Bedford, PA 15522
(814) 623-5174

Berwyn
Marriott Residence Inn   N/A   ***
600 W. Swedesford Road
Berwyn, PA 19312
(610) 640-9494

Bethlehem
Comfort Suites   G,H,R,SK   **
120 W. Third St.
Bethlehem, PA 18015
(610) 882-9700

Bensalem
Comfort Inn   G,H,R   **
3660 Street Rd.
Bensalem, PA 19020
(215) 245-0100

Blairsville
Comfort Inn   G,H,R,S   **
SR 22 E., Blairsville, PA 15717
(412) 459-7100

Bloomsburg
Quality Inn   R,T   *
1 Buckhorn Rd.
Bloomsburg, PA 17815
(717) 784-5300

MID-ATLANTIC

Breezewood
Comfort Inn   G,H,R,SK   *
US 30
Breezewood, PA 15533
(814) 735-2200

Brookville
HoJo Inn   R,NS   *
245 Allegheny Blvd.
Brookville, PA 15825
(814) 849-3335

Ramada Limited   G,R,S,NS   *
235 Allegheny Blvd
Brookville, PA 15825
(814) 849-8381

Carlisle
Econo Lodge   G,R,T   **
1460 Harrisburg Pike
Carlisle, PA 17013
(717) 249-7775

Quality Inn   H,R,S,NS   *
1255 Harrisburg Pike
Carlisle, PA 17013
(717) 243-6000

Chambersburg
Rodeway Inn   G,R,T,SK   *
1620 Lincoln Way E.
Chambersburg, PA 17201
(717) 264-4108

Chester
Howard Johnson Hotel   A,R,S,NS   *
1300 Providence Road
Chester, PA 19013
(610) 876-7211

MID-ATLANTIC

Clarion
Comfort Inn   G,H,R   **
Dolby St.
Clarion, PA 16214
(814) 226-5230

Delaware Water Gap
Glenwood Resort   G,T,SK   **
Main St., P.O. Box 159
Delaware Water Gap, PA 18327
(800) 833-3050; (717) 476-0010

Denver
Comfort Inn   G,H,R,T   *
2015 N. Reading Rd.
Denver, PA 17571
(717) 336-4649

Du Bois
Ramada Inn   G,H,R,S,NS,SA   *
I-80 Exit 17 & Route 255
Du Bois, PA 15801
(814) 371-7070

Ebensburg
Howard Johnson Lodge   H,R,NS   *
Route 22 West
Ebensburg, PA 15931
(814) 472-7201

Erie
Howard Johnson Lodge   R,S,NS   *
7575 Peach Street
Erie, PA 16509
(814) 864-4811

Gettysburg
Howard Johnson Lodge   H,S,NS   *
301 Steinwehr Avenue
Gettysburg, PA 17325
(717) 334-1188

(412) 459-7100

Holiday Inn Battlefield 516 Baltimore St. Gettysburg, PA 17325 (717) 334-6211	N/A	**

Hamlin

Comfort Inn I-84 & SR 191 Hamlin, PA 18436 (717) 689-4148	H,R,SA,SK	**

Harrisburg

Holiday Inn Route 441 & I-283 4751 Lindle Rd. Harrisburg, PA 17111 (800) 637-4817	R	**

Marriott Residence Inn 4480 Lewis Rd. Harrisburg, PA 17111 (717) 561-1900	S	***

Hawley

Martin's Cottages Hawley, PA (717) 226-9621	G,T,SK	**

Henryville

Alvin's Log Cabins Henryville, PA (717) 629-0667	G,T,SK	**

Horsham

Marriott Residence Inn 3 Walnut Grove Drive Horsham, PA 19044 (215) 443-7330	S,SA,R	***

MID-ATLANTIC

King of Prussia
Motel 6   G,R   *
815 W. DeKalb Pike
King of Prussia, PA 19406
(610) 265-7200

Lamar
Comfort Inn   G,H,R   *
I-80 at SR 64
Lamar, PA 16848
(717) 726-4901

Lancaster
Comfort Inn   G,R   *
500 Centerville Rd.
Lancaster, PA 17601
(717) 898-2431

Ramada Inn   A,G,R,S,T,NS,SK   *
2250 Lincln Hwy East
Lancanster, PA 17602
(717) 393-5499

Laureldale
Econo Lodge   G,R,T,SK   *
2310 Fraver Dr.
Laureldale, PA 19605
(610) 378-1145

Lester
Econo Lodge   G,R,T   *
600 SR 291
Lester, PA 19029
(215) 521-3900

Levittown
Comfort Inn   H,R   *
6401 Bristol Pk
Levittown, PA 19057
(215) 547-5000

MID-ATLANTIC

Lewisburg
Econo Lodge	G,R,T	*
US 15, Box 651		
Lewisburg, PA 17837		
(717) 523-1106		

Lititz
The General Sutter Inn	N/A	***
14 East Main St.		
Lititz, PA 17543		
(717) 626-2115		

Manheim
Rodeway Inn	G,R	*
2931 Lebanon Rd.		
Manheim, PA 17545		
(717) 665-2755		

Mansfield
Comfort Inn	G,H,R	**
300 Gateway Dr.		
Mansfield, PA 16933		
(717) 662-3000		

Matamoras
Best Western Inn	G,T,SK,R	**
900 Routes 6 & 209		
Matamoras, PA 18336		
(717) 491-2400; (800) 528-1234		

Mercer
Howard Johnson Lodge	H,R,S,NS	**
Rt. 19 & I-80 , RD #6		
Mercer, PA 16137		
(412) 748-3030		

New Castle
Comfort Inn	G,H,T,SA	**
1740 New Butler Rd.		
New Castle, PA 16101		
(412) 658-7700		

MID-ATLANTIC

New Columbia
Comfort Inn   G,H,R   *
I-80 & US 15
New Columbia, PA 17856
(717) 568-8000

Oakdale
Comfort Inn   G,R   **
7011 Old Steubenville Pike
Oakdale, PA 15071
(412) 787-2600

Howard Johnson Lodge   A,S,NS   *
2101 Montour Church Road
Oakdale, PA 15071
(412) 787-2244

Philadelphia
Best Western   A,H,R,S,NS   *
501 N. 22nd Street
Philadelphia, PA 19130
(215) 568-8300

Clarion Suites   A,H,NS   **
1010 Race St.
Philadelphia, PA 19107
(215) 922-1730

Marriott Residence Inn   S, SA   ***
4630 Island Avenue
Philadelphia, PA 19153
(215) 492-1611

Pine Grove
Comfort Inn   H,R,S   *
I-80 & SR 443
Pine Grove, PA 17963
(717) 345-8031

Econo Lodge   G,H,R,SK   *
RD 1, Box 581
Pine Grove, PA 17963
(717) 345-4099

Pittsburg
Econo Lodge   G,R,T   *
4800 Steubenville Pike
Pittsburg, PA 15205
(412) 922-6900

Best Western Hotel   R,S,NS   **
3401 Boulevard of Allies
Pittsburgh, PA 15213
(412) 683-6100

Howard Johnson Lodge   H,R,S,NS   **
5300 Clairton Boulevard
Pittsburgh, PA 15236
(412) 884-6000

Pittston
Howard Johnson Lodge   A,R,S,NS   *
307 Route 315
Pittston, PA 18640
(717) 654-3301

Punxatawney
Country Villa   N/A   ***
Route 119 South
Punxatawney, PA 15767
(814) 938-8330

Pantall Hotel   N/A   **
135 E. Mahoning St.
Punxsatawney, PA 15767
(814) 938-6600

MID-ATLANTIC

Scranton
Econo Lodge   H,R   **
1175 Kane St.
Scranton, PA 18505
(717) 348-1000

Selinsgrove
Comfort Inn   G,H,R   **
US 11/15
Selinsgrove, PA 17870
(717) 374-8880

Somerset
Ramada Inn   G,H,R,S,NS,SA,SK   *
PA Turnpike Exit 10
Somerset, PA 15501
(814) 443-4646

Stroudsberg
Colony Motor Lodge   G,T,SK   **
1863 W, Main St.
Stroudsberg, PA
(717) 421-3790

Budget Motor Lodge   G,T,SK   **
I-80 Exit 51
East Stroudsberg, PA 18301
(800) 233-8144

Tannersville
HoJo Inn   H,R,S,NS   *
Rte. 715 and I-80
Tannersville, PA 18372
(717) 629-4100

York
Ramada Inn   G,H,R,S,NS,SA   *
1650 Toronita St.
York, PA 17402
(717) 846-4940

MID-ATLANTIC

Waynesburg
Econo Lodge   G,H,R,T   *
350 Miller Ln.
Waynesburg, PA 15370
(412) 627-5544

West Middlesex
Comfort Inn   G,H,S,SA   **
SR 18 & Wilson Rd.
West Middlesex, PA 16159
(412) 342-7200

White Haven
Mountain Laurel Resort   G,T,SK,R   ***
I-80 at Northeast Ext.
White Haven, PA 18661
(717) 443-8411

Williamsport
Econo Lodge   R   *
2401 E. Third St.
Williamsport, PA 17701
(717) 326-1501

Wyomissing
Econo Lodge   G,H,R   *
635 Spring St.
Wyomissing, PA 19610
(610) 378-5105

VIRGINIA (See DC listings for Washington suburbs)

Ashland
Comfort Inn   G,H,R,SA   *
101 Cottage Greene Dr.
Ashland, VA 23005
(804) 752-7777

Blacksburg
Comfort Inn   G,H,R   *
3705 S. Main St.
Blacksburg, VA 24060
(540) 951-1500

Bristol
Red Carpet Inn   R,S,NS   *
I-81 Exit 10, 4766 Lee Hwy
Bristol, VA 24201
(540) 669-1151

Charlottesville
Comfort Inn   G,H,R,T,SK   **
1807 Emmet St.
Charlottesville, VA 22901
(804) 293-6188

Econo Lodge   G,R,T   *
2041 Holiday Dr.
Charlottesville, VA 22901
(804) 295-3185

Marriott Residence Inn   S   ***
1111 Millmont Street
Charlottesville, VA 22901
(800) 331-3131 (Opening Spring 1997)

Christiansburg
Econo Lodge   H,R   *
2430 Roanoke St.
Christiansburg, VA 24073
(540) 382-6161

HoJo Inn   H,NS   *
100 Bristol Drive
Christiansburg, VA 24073
(540) 381-0150

Covington
Comfort Inn   H,R,SK   **
SR 5, Mallow Rd.
Covington, VA 24426
(540) 962-2141

Culpepper
Comfort Inn   G,H,R,T   *
890 Willis Ln.
Culpepper, VA 22701
(540) 825-4900

Emporia
Comfort Inn   H,R   *
1411 Skippers Rd.
Emporia, VA 23847
(804) 348-3282

Fredericksburg
Econo Lodge   G,H,R   *
5321 Jefferson Davis Hwy.
Fredericksburg, VA 22408
(540) 898-5440

Howard Johnson Lodge   R,S,NS   *
5327 Jefferson Davis Hwy.
Fredericksburg, VA 22408
(540) 898-1800

Ramada Inn Spotsylvania Mall   G,H,R,S,NS   *
I-95, Exit 130B, PO Box 36
Fredericksburg, VA 22404
(540) 786-8361

Hampton
Econo Lodge   G,R,T   *
2708 W. Mercury Blvd.
Hampton, VA 23666
(757) 826-8970

MID-ATLANTIC

Quality Inn   G,H,R,S   **
1215 W. Mercury Blvd.
Hampton, VA 23666
(757) 838-5011

Harrisonburg
Comfort Inn   G,H,R,SK   *
1440 E. Market St.
Harrisonburg, VA 22801
(540) 433-6066

Econo Lodge   H,R,SK   *
US 33 & I-81
Harrisonburg, VA 22801
(540) 433-2576

HoJo Inn   H,R,S,NS   *
605 Port Republic Rd
Harrisonburg, VA 22801
(540) 434-6771

Ramada Inn   G,H,R,S,T,NS,SK   *
1 Pleasant Valley Rd.
Harrisonburg, VA 22801
(540) 434-9981

Hillsville
Econo Lodge   G,H,R,T   **
I-77 & US 58
Hillsville, VA 24343
(540) 728-9118

Lexington
Comfort Inn   H,R,T,S   *
I-64 & US 11
Lexington, VA 24450
(540) 463-7311

Howard Johnson Hotel   R,S,NS   *
I-64/O-81 at US 11
Lexington, VA 24450
(540) 463-9181

Ramada Inn   G,H,R,S,NS   *
Hwy 11 at I-81, Exit 195
Lexington, VA 24450
(540) 463-6666

Lynchburg
Comfort Inn   G,H,R,T   **
US 29 Expwy., Odd Fellows Rd.
Lynchburg, VA 24501
(804) 847-9041

Howard Johnson Lodge   H,R,S,NS   *
US Rt 29 North, PO Box 10729
Lynchburg, VA 24506
(804) 845-7041

Newport News
Ramada Inn   A,G,H,R,S,T,NS   *
950 J Clyde Morris Blvd
Newport News, VA 23601
(757) 599-4460

Norfolk
Comfort Inn   H,R,SA   *
930 Virginia Beach Blvd.
Norfolk, VA 23504
(757) 623-5700

Econo Lodge   G,H,R,T,SA   *
9601 4th View St.
Norfolk, VA 23503
(757) 480-9611

Howard Johnson Hotel   R,S,NS   *
700 Monticello Avee
Norfolk, VA 23510
(757) 627-5555

Ramada Inn City Center 2   H,R,NS   *
Freemason & Granby Streets
Norfolk, VA 23510
(757) 622-6682

MID-ATLANTIC

Petersburg
Econo Lodge   G,H,R,T   *
16905 Parkdale Rd.
Petersburg, VA 23805
(804) 862-2717

Richmond
Marriott Residence Inn   S,SA   ***
2121 Dickens Road
Richmond, VA 23230
(804) 285-8200

Roanoke
Ramada Inn-Roanoke Central   A,G,H,R,S,T,NS   **
1927 Franklin Rd.
Roanoke, VA 24014
(540) 343-0121

Smithfield
Four Square Plantation   N/A   **
13357 Four Square Road
Smithfield, VA
(757) 365-0749

Troutville
Howard Johnson Lodge   H,R,S,NS   *
PO Box 100
Troutville, VA 24175
(540) 992-3000

Warrenton
HoJo Inn   R,S,NS   *
6 Broadview Avenue
Warrenton, VA 22186
(540) 347-4141

Williamsburg
Sheraton   A,G,H,S,NS   *
351 York Street
Williamsburg, VA 23185
(757) 229-4100

Ramada Inn Ewell Station   A,G,R,S,T,NS   *
5351 Richmond Road
Williamsburg, VA 23185
(757) 565-2000

Williamsburg Woodlands   R,S   ***
102 Visitor's Center Drive
Williamsburg, VA 23185
(804) 253-2277

Governor's Inn   R,S   ***
506 North Henry Street
Williamsburg, VA
(804) 253-2277

Wytheville
Shenandoah Inn   H,R,S,NS   *
I-81 & I-77 & US 52
Wytheville, VA 24382
(540) 228-3188

Ramada Inn   G,H,R,S,T,NS   *
Intersection of I-81
955 Pepper's Ferry Rd.
Wytheville, VA 24382
(540) 228-6000

WEST VIRGINIA

Beckley
Comfort Inn   H,R,T,SK   *
1909 Harper Rd.
Beckley, WV 25801
(304) 255-2161

Charleston
Ramada Inn   A,H,R,S,NS   *
2nd Ave & B Street
Charleston, WV 25303
(304) 744-4641

MID-ATLANTIC

Elkins
Econo Lodge   G,R,S   *
RT 1, Box 15
Elkins, WV 26241
(304) 636-5311

Morgantown
Ramada Inn   A,G,H,R,S,NS   *
PO Box 1242
Morgantown, WV 26505
(304) 296-3431

Sistersville
The Hotel at the Wells Inn   G,T,R   *
316 Charles St.
Sistersville, WV 26175
(304) 652-1312

Summersville
Sleep Inn   G,H,R,T   *
701 Professional Park Dr.
Summersville, WV 26651
(304) 872-4500

Wheeling
Comfort Inn   G,T,R,S   *
I-70
Wheeling, WV
(304) 547-1380

Days Inn   G,T,R,S   *
I-70
Wheeling, WV
(304) 547-0610

Oglebay Resort   G,T,H,R,S   **
Route 88N
Wheeling WV 26003
(800) 624-6988 (cabins only)

SOUTHEAST

SOUTHEAST

Alabama
Florida
Georgia
Mississippi
North Carolina
South Carolina
Tennessee

Hotel Cost Codes (for average one-night stay)

*	$30-60/night
**	$61-100/night
***	$101-150/night
****	$151 and up/night
W	Hotel has weekly rates only

Note: costs may vary by season.

Hotel Amenity Codes

A	Airport nearby
H	Handicapped access
HS	Hair salon on premises
G	Golf within 10 miles
NS	Non-smoking rooms available
OB	Facility is on the beach
P	Playground on premises
R	Restaurant on premises
S	Swimming on premises
SA	Sauna on premises
SK	Skiing within 25 miles
T	Tennis within 10 miles

ALABAMA

Anniston
Ramada Inn   S,A,G,R,NS   *
300 Quintard Ave.
Anniston, AL 36201
(205) 237-9777

Auburn
Quality Inn   G,H,R,T   *
1577 S. College St.
Auburn, AL 36830
(205) 821-7001

Bessemer
Best Western   H,R   *
1098 Ninth Avenue SW
Bessemer, AL 35021
(800) 528-1234

Ramada/Days Inn   H   **
1021 9th Ave. SW
Bessemer, AL 35023
(205) 424-9780

Birmingham
Marriott Residence Inn   G, T   **
State Farm Pkwy.
Birhamington, AL 35209
(800) 331-3131

Clanton
Rodeway Inn   G,R   *
2301 7th St.
Clanton, AL 35045
(205) 755-4049

Collinsville
HoJo Inn   NS,H,R,S   *
I-59 & Hwy 68, Exit 205
Collinsville, AL 35961
(205) 524-2114

Cullman
Ramada Inn   S,H,G,T,R,NS   **
I-65 & Hwy 69
1600 County Rd.437
Cullman, AL 35056-1204
(205) 734-8484

Howard Johnson Lodge   NS,R,S   *
I-65 & Hwy 278W, Exit 308
Cullman, AL 35056
(205) 737-7275

Daleville
Econo Lodge   H,R   *
241 Daleville Ave.
Daleville, AL 36322
(334) 598-6304

Dauphin Island
Gulf Breeze Motel   N/A   **
1512 Cadillac Ave.
Dauphin Island, AL 36528
(205) 861-7344

Decatur
Ramada Inn   S,H,G,T,P,NS   *
1317 Hwy 67
Decatur, AL 35602
(205) 353-0333

Sterling Inn   NS,R   *
440 Johnson Street, SE
Decatur, AL 35601-3008
(205) 355-8504

Motor Lodge   H,R   **
3429 US 31 S.
Decatur, AL 35601
(205) 355-0190

Dothan
Comfort Inn   G,H,R,T   **
3591 Ross Clark Cir.
Dothan, AL 36304
(334) 793-9090

Ramada Inn   S,A,H,G,T,NS   *
3011 Ross Clark Circle
(231 By-Pass)
Dothan, AL 36301
(334) 792-0031

Evergreen
Comfort Inn   H,R   *
Bates Rd., P.O. Box 564
Evergreen, AL 36401
(205) 578-4701

Florence
Knights Inn   A,NS,H,R,S   *
1241 Florence Blvd.
Florence, AL 35630
(205) 764-5421

Greenville
Econo Lodge   G,H,R,T   *
946 Fort Dale Rd.
Greenville, AL 36037
(205) 382-3118

Gulf Shores
Beachview   OB,NS,R   *
200 E. Beach Blvd
Gulf Shores, AL 36542
(334) 948-6844

SOUTHEAST

Heflin
HoJo Inn   NS,H,R   *
Route 2, Box 44T
Heflin, AL 36264
(205) 463-2900

Huntsville
Knights Inn   NS,S,R   *
4404 University Dr.
Huntsville, AL 35816
(205) 837-3250

Marriott Residence Inn   N/A   **
4020 Independence Drive
Huntsville, AL 35816
(205) 837-8907

Mobile
Ramada Inn   S,H,G,T,NS   *
Battleship Pkwy.
P.O. Box 1626
Mobile, AL 36633
(334) 626-7200

Howard Johnson Lodge   NS,H,R,S,T   *
3132 Government Boulevard
I-65 & US 90
Mobile, AL 36606
(334) 471-2402

Econo Lodge   G,H,R,T   *
1 S. Beltline Hwy.
Mobile, AL 36606
(334) 479-5333

Clarion Hotel   G,H,R   **
3101 Airport Blvd.
Mobile, AL 36606
(334) 476-6400

SOUTHEAST

Montgomery
Econo Lodge   G,H,R,T   *
4135 Troy Hwy.
Montgomery, AL 36116
(334) 284-3400

Governor's House Hotel   NS,H,R,S   *
2705 E. South Blvd
Montgomery, AL 36116
(334) 288-2800

Oxford
Howard Johnson Lodge   H,R,S,NS   *
PO Box 3308, Oxford
Oxford, AL 36203
(205) 835-3988

Vestavia Hills
Howard Johnson Hotel   NS,H,R,S,T   *
1485 Montgomery Highway
Vestavia Hills, AL 35216
(205) 823-4300

FLORIDA

Apollo Beach
Ramada Bayside   G,R,S,NS,OB   *
6414 Surfside Blvd
Apollo Beach, FL 33572
(813) 641-2700

Boca Raton
Marriott Residence Inn   A,G,T   ***
525 NW 77th St.
Boca Raton, FL 33487
(561) 994-3222

Bonifay
Econo Lodge   H,R,T   **
2210 S. Waukesha St.
Bonifay, FL 32425
(904) 547-9345

Bradenton
Econo Lodge   G,R,T   *
6727 14th St.
Bradenton, FL 34207
(941) 758-7199

Callahan
Friendship Inn   G,H,R,T   *
US 1 & US 23 N.
Callahan, FL 32011
(904) 879-3451

Cape Coral
Quality Inn   G,H,T   *
1538 Cape Coral Pkwy.
Cape Coral, FL 33904
(941) 542-2121

Coral Gables
Howard Johnson Lodge   R,S,NS   *
1430 South Dixie Highway
Coral Gables, FL 33146
(305) 665-7501

Crystal River
Comfort Inn   G,R,T   *
4486 N. Suncoast`Blvd.
Crystal River, FL 34428
(352) 563-1500

Cocoa
Econo Lodge   G,R   *
3220 N. Cocoa Blvd.
Cocoa, FL 32926
(407) 632-4561

SOUTHEAST

Ramada Inn Cocoa   G,H,R,S,NS   **
900 Friday Road
I-95 at Exit 76
Cocoa, FL 32926
(407) 631-1210

Cocoa Beach
Best Western   G,H,R,T   *
5500 N. Atlantic Ave.
Cocoa Beach, FL 32931
(407) 784-2550

Deerfield Beach
Comfort Inn   G,H,R   **
1040 E. Newport Center Dr.
Deerfield Beach, FL 33442
(954) 570-8887

Quality Suites   G,R   **
1050 E. Newport Center Dr.
Deerfield Beach, FL 33442
(954) 570-8888

DeFuniak Springs
Comfort Inn   G,H,R,T   *
1326 S. Freeport Rd.
DeFuniak Springs, FL 32433
(904) 892-1333

Days Inn   G,H,R   **
1325 South Freeport Rd.
DeFuniak Springs, FL 32433
(904) 892-6115

De Land
Quality Inn   H,R   *
I-4 & SR 44
2801 E. New York Ave.
De Land, FL 32724
(904) 736-3440

SOUTHEAST

Dunedin
Sail Winds   G,R,T   **
1414 Bayshore Blvd.
Dunedin, FL 34698
(813) 734-8851

Elkton
Comfort Inn   G,H,R   *
2625 SR 207
Elkton, FL 32033
(904) 829-3435

Fort Pierce
Howard Johnson   A,H,R,S,NS   *
7150 Okeechobee Road
Fort Pierce, FL 34945
(407) 464-4500

Ft. Walton Beach
Howard Johnson Lodge   H,S,NS   *
314 Miracle Strip Parkway
Fort Walton Beach, FL 32548
(904) 243-6162

Gainesville
Marriott Inn   A,SA   ***
4001 SW 13th St.
Gainesville, FL 32608
(352) 371-2101

Haines City
Econo Lodge   G,R,T   *
1504 US 27 S.
Haines City, FL 33844
(813) 422-8621

Homestead
Howard Johnson Lodge   R,S,NS   *
1020 North Homestead Blvd.
Homestead, FL 33030
(305) 248-2121

Jacksonville
Comfort Suites 8333 Dix Ellis Trail Jacksonville, FL 32256 (904) 739-1155	G,H,R	*
Comfort Inn 3233 Emerson St. Jacksonville, FL 32207 (904) 398-3331	H,R	**
Ramada Inn South 2 5624 Cagle Road Jacksonville, FL 32216 (904) 737-8000	G,H,R,S,NS	*
Ramada Inn East 3 6237 Arlington Expwy Jacksonville, FL 32211 (904) 725-5093	G,H,R,S,NS	*
Ramada Inn Mandarin 4 Conference Center 3130 Hartley Rd I-295 & St Rt 13, Exit 2, Jacksonville, FL 32257 (904) 268-8080	G,H,R,S,NS	*
Marriott Inn Off I-95 8365 Dix Ellis Trail Jacksonville, FL 32256 (904) 733-8088	N/A	***

Jennings
Rodemaster I-75 & SR 143, Rt. 1 Jennings, FL 32053 (904) 938-5500	H,R,SA	*

SOUTHEAST

Kendall
Howard Johnson Lodge   R,S,NS   **
10201 South Dixie Hwy
Kendall, FL 33156
(305) 666-2531

Key Largo
Howard Johnson Resort Lodge   H,R,S,NS,OB   **
Route 1, Mile Marker 102
Key Largo, FL 33037
(305) 451-1400

Key West
Ramada Inn Key West   A,G,H,R,S,NS,SA   **
3420 N Roosevelt Blvd
Key West, FL 33040
(305) 294-5541

Kissimmee
Comfort Inn   G,H,R,T   *
7571 W. Irlo Bronson Hwy.
Kissimmee, FL 34747
(407) 396-7500

Holiday Inn East-Main Gate   R   ***
5678 W. Irlo Bronson Mem. Hwy
Kissimmee, FL 34746
(407) 396-4488

Howard Johnson Lodge   H,S,NS   *
2323 Highway 192
East Kissimmee, FL 32743
(407) 846-4900

Ramada Inn 192   G,H,R,S,NS   *
Disney Area East 11
4559 West Highway 192
Kissimmee, FL 34746
(407) 396-1212

Ramada Limited   G,H,S,NS   *
Disney Area East 12
5055 West Highway 192
Kissimmee, FL 34746
(407) 396-2212

Lachua
Ramada Limited   H,S,NS   *
Rt. 1/Box 225B
I-75 & US 441/Ext 78A
Lachua, FL 32615
(904) 462-4200

Lake Buena Vista
Comfort Inn   G,H,R,T   *
8442 Palm Pkwy
Lake Buena Vista, FL 32836
(407) 239-7300

Lake City
Econo Lodge   G,H,R,T   *
I-75 & US 90
Lake City, FL 32055
(904) 752-7891

Rodeway Inn   G,H,R,T   *
I-75 & US 90
Lake City, FL 32056
(904) 755-5203

Howard Johnson Lodge   H,R,S,NS   *
Route 13, Box 1082
Lake City, FL 32055
(904) 752-6262

Ramada Inn   A,G,H,R,S,NS,SA   *
Rt 13, Box 1075
Lake City, FL 32055
(904) 752-7550

SOUTHEAST

Lakeland
Comfort Inn   G,H,R   *
1817 E. Memorial Blvd.
Lakeland, FL 33801
(941) 688-9221

Live Oak
Econo Lodge   G,H,R   *
US 129 & I-10
Live Oak, FL 32060
(904) 362-7459

Macclenny
Econo Lodge   G,H,R   *
I-10 & SR 121
Macclenny, FL 32063
(904) 259-3000

Marathon
Howard Johnson Lodge   A,H,R,S,NS   *
13351 Overseas Highway
Marathon, FL 33050
(305) 743-8550

Melbourne
Travel Lodge   G,R,T   *
4505 W. New Haven Ave.
Melbourne, FL 32904
(407) 724-5450

Quality Suites   G,R,SA   **
1665 SR A1A N
Melbourne, FL 32903
(407) 723-4222

Miami
Paramount Hotel   A,H,R,S,NS   **
1980 Northwest LeJeune Road
Miami, FL 33126
(305) 871-4370

SOUTHEAST

Marriott Inn   S,A   ***
1212 NW 82nd Ave.
Miami, FL 33126
(305) 591-2211

Howard Johnson Lodge   H,R,S,NS   *
7330 Northwest 36th Street
Miami, FL 33166
(305) 592-5440

Ramada Limited   A,G,H,S,NS   *
7600 N Kendall Drive
Miami, FL 33156
(305) 595-6000

Quality Inn   G,R,T   **
14501 D. Dixie Hwy.
Miami, FL 33176
(305) 251-2000

Niceville
Friendship Inn   G,H,R,T   *
626 John Sims Pkwy.
Niceville, FL 32578
(904) 678-4164

Ocala
Quality Inn   G,R   *
3767 N.W. Blitchton Rd.
Ocala, FL 34475
(352) 732-2300

Orlando
Econo Lodge   G,R,T   *
3300 W. Colonial Dr.
Orlando, FL 32808
(407) 293-7221

Howard Johnson Lodge   R,S,NS   *
6603 International Drive
Orlando, FL 32819
(407) 351-2900

SOUTHEAST

Howard Johnson Plaza-Hotel 3835 McCoy Road Orlando, FL 32812 (407) 859-2711	A,R,S,NS	*
La Quinta Inn Disney Area 1 8300 Jamaican Court Orlando, FL 32819 (407) 351-1660	A,G,H,R,S,NS	*
Quality Inn 9000 International Dr. Orlando, FL 32819 (407) 345-8585	G,H,R,T	*
Quality Inn 7600 International Dr. Orlando, FL 32819 (407) 351-1600	G,H,R,T	*
Marriott Inn 270 Douglas Ave. Orlando, FL 32714 (407) 788-7991	S,SA,G	***

Ormond Beach

Comfort Inn 507 S. Atlantic Ave. Ormond Beach, FL 32074 (904) 677-8550	G,H,R,T	*
Budget Host Inn 1633 North US 1 & I-95 Ormond Beach, FL 32174 (904) 677-7310	H,S,NS	*

Palm Harbor

Travel Lodge 32000 US 19 N. Palm Harbor, FL 34684 (813) 786-2529	G,H,R,T	*

SOUTHEAST

Pensacola
Comfort Inn   G,H,R   *
3 New Warrington Rd.
Pensacola, FL 32506
(904) 455-3233

Comfort Inn   G,H,R   *
6919 Pensacola Blvd.
Pensacola, FL 32505
(904) 478-4499

HoJo Inn   S,NS   *
4126 Mobile Hwy.
Pensacola, FL 32506
(904) 456-5731

Sanibel Island
Carribe Beach Resort   G,T   ***
2669 W. Gulf Dr., P.O. Box 158
Sanibel Island, FL 33957
(813) 472-1166; (800) 237-7370

Signal Beach & Club   G,T   ***
1811 Olde Middle Gulf Dr.
Sanibel Island, FL 33957
(813) 472-4690

Mitchell's Sand Castle   G,T   ***
3951 W. Gulf Dr.
Sanibel Island, FL 33957
(813) 472-1282

Sarasota
Comfort Inn   G,H,R,T   *
8440 N. Tamiami Trail
Sarasota, FL 34243
(941) 355-7771

Howard Johnson   G,H,R,T   *
811 S. Tamiami Trail
Sarasota, FL 34237
(813) 365-0350

SOUTHEAST

St. Augustine
Econo Lodge   G,H,R   *
2535 SR 16
St. Augustine, FL 32092
(904) 829-5643

Super 8   H,R,S,NS   *
2550 State Road 16
St. Augustine, FL 32085
(904) 829-5686

Howard Johnson Resort Hotel   R,S,NS,OB   *
2050 A1A South
St. Augustine, FL 32084
(904) 471-2575

Ramada Inn   G,H,R,S,T,NS   *
116 San Marco Avenue
St. Augustine, FL 32084
(904) 824-4352

St. Petersburg
Marriott Inn   N/A   ***
5050 Ulmerton Rd.
Clearwater, FL 34620
(813) 573-4444

Siesta Key
Turtle Beach Resort   S,G   ***
9049 Midnight Pass Rd.
Siesta Key, FL 34242
(941) 349-4554

Tallahassee
Econo Lodge   G,H,R,T   *
2681 N. Monroe St.
Tallahassee, FL 32303
(904) 385-6155

Tampa

Econo Lodge	G,R	*

2905 N. 50th St.
Tampa, FL 33619
(813) 621-3541

Econo Lodge	G,R,T	*

1701 E. Busch Blvd.
Tampa, FL 33612
(813) 933-7681

Econo Lodge	G,R	*

1020 S. Dale Mabry
Tampa, FL 33629
(813) 254-3005

Howard Johnson Lodge	R,S,NS	*

4139 E. Busch Blvd.
Tampa, FL 33617
(813) 988-9191

Howard Johnson Lodge	A,H,R,S,NS	*

2055 N. Dale Mabry
Tampa, FL 33607
(813) 875-8818

Holiday Inn USF 2	G,H,R,S,T,NS	*

I-275 Exit 36, 400 E Bearss Avenue
Tampa, FL 33613
(813) 961-1000

Titusville

Howard Johnson Lodge	H,S,NS	*

1829 Riverside Drive
Titusville, FL 32780
(407) 267-7900

Treasure Island

Lorelei Resort	S	**

10273 Gulf Blvd.
Treasure Island, FL 33706
(800) 354-6364; (813) 360-4351

SOUTHEAST

Vero Beach
HoJo Inn   R,NS   *
1985 90th Avenue
Vero Beach, FL 32966
(407) 778-1985

West Palm Beach
Comfort Inn   G,H,R,T   **
1901 Palm Beach Lakes Blvd.
West Palm Beach, FL 33409
(407) 689-6100

Comfort Inn   G,H,R,T   *
5981 Okeechobee Blvd.
West Palm Beach, FL 33417
(407) 697-3388

Winter Haven
Howard Johnson Lodge   H,R,S,NS   *
1300 3rd Street Southwest
Winter Haven,FL 33880
(941) 294-7321

Camping Information:
Florida Campground Association
1638 N. Plaza Dr.
Tallahassee, FL 32308
(904) 656-8878

GEORGIA

Acworth
Ramada Limited   S,NS   *
164 North Pointway
I-75 & Hwy 92, Exit 120 at I-75
Acworth, GA 30102
(770) 975-9000

Quality Inn   G,H,R   **
4980 Cowan Rd.
Acworth, GA 30101
(770) 974-1922

Adel
HoJo Inn   H,R,S,NS   *
I-75 Exit 10, 1103 West 4th St
Adel, GA 31620
(912) 896-2244

Albany
Econo Lodge   H,R   *
1806 E.Oglethorpe Blvd.
Albany, GA 31705
(912) 883-5544

Ramada Inn   N/A   **
1505 N Slappey Blvd
Albany, GA 31701
(912) 883-3211

Atlanta area
Beverly Hills Inn   G   **
65 Sheridan Drive NE
Atlanta, GA 30305
(404) 233-8520

Quality Inn   R,SA   **
330 Peachtree Street
Atlanta, GA 30308
(404) 577-1980

Marriott Inn   A   ***
3401 Int'l Blvd.
Hapeville, GA 30354
(404) 761-0511

Marriott Inn   A   ***
5465 Windward Pkwy
Alpharetta, GA 30201
(770) 664-0664

SOUTHEAST

Marriott Inn 2960 Piedmont Rd. Atlanta, GA 30305 (404) 239-0677	A	***
Marriott Inn 2771 Hargrove Rd. Smyrna, GA 30080 (770) 433-8877	A	***
Marriott Inn 1901 Savoy Drive Atlanta, GA 30341 (770) 455-4446	A	***
Marriott Inn George Busby Pkwy. Kennesaw, GA 30144 (800) 331-3131	A	***

Athens

Ramada Inn 513 W. Broad Street Athens, GA 30601 (706) 546-8122	A,G,H,R,S,T,NS	*

Augusta

HoJo Inn 1238 Gordon Highway Augusta, GA 30901 (706) 724-9613	A,H,R,S,NS	*

Brunswick

Comfort Inn 5272 New Jessup Hwy. Brunswick, GA 31525 (912) 261-0670	G,H,R,T	*
Howard Johnson Lodge I-95 and Highway 341 Brunswick, GA 31520 (912) 264-4720	R,S,NS	*

SOUTHEAST

Ramada Inn Downtown 3241 Glynn Avenue Brunswick, GA 31523 (912) 264-8611	A,G,H,S,T,NS	*
Ramada Inn I-95 Exit 7A, I-95 & US 341 Brunswick, GA 31520 (912) 264-3621	A,G,H,R,S,NS	*
Sleep Inn 5272 New Jessup Hwy. Brunswick, GA 31525 (912) 261-0670	G,H,R	*

Byron

Econo Lodge I-75 Exit 46 Byron, GA 31008 (912) 956-5600	G,R,T	*

Calhoun

Quality Inn 915 SR 53 East Calhoun, GA 30701 (706) 629-9501	G,H,R	*

Cartersville

Comfort Inn 28 SR 294 Cartersville, GA 30120 (770) 387-1800	G,H,R	**
Econo Lodge White-Cassville Rd. Cartersville, GA 30120 (770) 386-0700	G,R	**
Econo Lodge I-75 N. at exit 125 Cartersville, GA 30120 (770) 386-3303	G,H,R,T	**

SOUTHEAST

Columbus
Comfort Inn   G,H,R,T   *
3443 Macron Rd.
Columbus, GA 31907
(706) 568-3300

Econo Lodge   G,H,R   *
4483 Victory Dr.
Columbus, GA 31903
(706) 682-3803

Commerce
HoJo Inn   R,S,NS   *
I-85 & US 441, Exit 53
Commerce, GA 30529
(706) 335-5581

Ramada Limited   H,S,NS   *
US Hwy 441 and I-85
Commerce, GA 30529
(706) 335-5191

Cordele
Rodeway Inn   G,R,T   *
1609 16th Ave. E.
Cordele, GA 31015
(912) 273-3390

Ramada Inn   G,R,S,T,NS   *
I-75, Ex. 33
2016 16th Ave. E
Cordele, GA 31015
(912) 273-5000

Dalton
Howard Johnson Lodge   H,R,S,NS   *
2107 Chattanooga Road
Dalton, GA 30720
(706) 278-1448

Doraville
Comfort Inn   H,R   **
2001 Clearview Ave.
Doraville, GA 30340
(404) 455-1811

Jekyll Island
Clarion Resort   G,H,R   **
85 S. Beachview Dr.
Jekyll Island, GA 31527
(912) 635-2261

Comfort Inn   G,H,R,T   **
711 Beachview Dr.
Jekyll Island, GA 31527
(912) 635-2211

Kennesaw
Comfort Inn   G,H,R   **
750 Cobb Place Blvd.
Kennesaw, GA 30144
(770) 419-1530

Kingsland
Comfort Inn   H,R,SA   **
I-95 & SR 40
Kingsland, GA 31548
(912) 729-6979

Quality Inn   G,H,R,S,NS   *
I-95, Exit 2
985 Boone Street
Kingsland, GA 31548
(912) 729-4363

Macon
Comfort Inn   G,R,T   *
2690 Riverside Dr.
Macon, GA 31204
(912) 746-8855

SOUTHEAST

HoJo Inn   R,S,NS   *
4709 Chambers Road
Macon, GA 31206
(912) 781-6680

Howard Johnson Lodge   H,R,S,NS   *
2566 Riverside Drive
Macon, GA 31204
(912) 746-7671

Rodeway Inn   G,R,T   *
4999 Eisenhower Pkwy.
Macon, GA 31206
(912) 781-4343

Quality Inn   G,H,R   *
4630 Chamber Rd.
Macon, GA 31206
(912) 781-7000

Norcross
Comfort Inn   G,H,R   *
5990 Western Hills Dr.
Norcross, GA 30071
(404) 368-0218

Perry
Rodeway Inn   G,R,T   *
103 Marshallville Rd.
Perry,GA 31069
(912) 987-3200

Regency Inn   R,S,NS   *
405 General Hodges Blvd.
Perry, GA 31069
(912) 987-7747

Quality Inn   H,R   *
I-75 at US 341
Perry, GA 31069
(912) 987-1345

Pooler

Ramada Inn Conference Center   A,H,R,S,NS,SA   *
Savannah Airport 2
301 Governor Treutlen Drive
Pooler, GA 31332
(912) 748-6464

Richmond Hill

Econo Lodge   G,R   *
I-95 & US 17 S.
Richmond Hill, GA 31324
(912) 756-3312

Savannah

Marriott Inn   S,SA   ***
5710 White Bluff Rd.
Savannah, GA 31405
(912) 356-3266

Bed & Breakfast Inn   G,R,T   **
117 W. Gordon St.
Savannah, GA 31401
(912) 238-0518

Econo Lodge   G,R,T   *
7 Gateway Blvd.
Savannah, GA 31419
(912) 925-2280

Quality Inn   G,H,R,T   **
1130 Bob Harmon Rd.
Savannah, GA 31408
(912) 964-1421

Thomasville

Susina Plantation Inn   R,S,G   ***
Route 3, Box 1010
Thomasville, GA 31792
(912) 377-9644

SOUTHEAST

Shoney's Inn   R,G   *
305 Hwy 195
Thomasville, GA 31792
(912) 228-5555

Tifton
Comfort Inn   G,H,R,S,T   *
1104 King Rd.
Tifton, GA 31794
(912) 382-4410

Ramada Inn   A,G,R,S,T,NS   *
I-75 & US 82 (Exit 18)
PO Box 1450
Tifton, GA 31793
(912) 382-8500

Best Western   H,R,T   *
1103 King Rd.
Tifton, GA 31794
(912) 386-2100

Valdosta
Comfort Inn   H,R   *
I-75 & US 84
Valdosta, GA 31601
(912) 242-1212

Days Inn   H,R,S,NS   *
North Valdosta Rd.
Valdosta, GA 31602
(912) 244-4460

Ramada Inn   A,G,R,S,NS   *
I-75 & GA 84
Valdosta, GA 31601
(912) 242-1225

Quality Inn   G,H,R   *
1902 W. Hill Ave.
Valdosta, GA 31601
(912) 244-4520

SOUTHEAST

Quality Inn   G,H,R,T   *
I-75 & US 94
Valdosta, GA 31601
(912) 244-8510

MISSISSIPPI

Brookhaven
Ramada Inn   H,R,S,NS   *
1210 Brookway Blvd.
Brookhaven, MS 39601
(601) 833-1341

Corinth
Comfort Inn   H,R   *
US 72 & 45
Corinth, MS 38834
(601) 287-4421

Forest
Comfort Inn   H,R   *
1250 SR 35 S.
Forest, MS 39074
(601) 469-2100

Greenville
Ramada Inn   G,H,R,S,NS   *
2700 US 82 East
Greenville, MS 38701
(601) 332-4411

Greenwood
Comfort Inn   G,H,R,T   *
410 US 82 W.
Greenwood, MS 38930
(601) 453-5974

Ramada Inn   A,G,H,R,S,T,NS   *
900 W Park Ave
Greenwood, MS 38930
(601) 455-2321

Hattiesburg
Comfort Inn   H,R,S,NS   *
6595 Hwy 49 North
Hattiesburg, MS 39401
(601) 268-2170

Ramada Limited   A,G,H,R,S,T,NS   *
900 Broadway Drive
Hattiesburg, MS 39401
(601) 582-7101

Jackson
Rodeway Inn   G,H,R   *
5925 I-55 N.
Jackson, MS 39121
(601) 373-1244

Marriott Residence Inn   N/A   ***
881 E. River Place
Jackson, MS 39202
(601) 355-3599

Ramada Inn Coliseum 1   A,G,H,R,S,NS   *
400 Greymont Ave
Jackson, MS 39202
(601) 969-2141

Ramada Plaza Hotel 3   A,G,H,S,T,HS,NS   *
1001 County Line Road
Jackson, MS 39211
(601) 957-2800

Northside Inn   G,H,R,T   *
4641 I-55 N.
Jackson, MS 39206
(601) 982-1044

SOUTHEAST

McComb
Best Western   G,H,S,T,NS   *
I-55 at Delaware Ave
PO Box 1460
McComb, MS 39648
(601) 684-5566

Meridian
Econo Lodge   G,H,R,T   *
2405 S. Frontage Rd.
Meridian, MS 39301
(601) 693-9393

Natchez
Howard Johnson Lodge   H,R,S,NS   *
Hwy. 61 South
Natchez, MS 39120
(601) 442-1691

Senatobia
Senatobia Inn   H,R,S,NS   *
501 E. Main Street
Senatobia, MS 38668
(601) 562-5241

Tupelo
Econo Lodge   H,R   *
1500 McCullough Blvd.
Tupelo, MS 38801
(601) 844-1901

Vicksburg
Ramada Limited   G,S,T,NS,OB   *
4216 Washington St.
Vicksburg, MS 39180
(601) 638-5750

The Corners   G,S,T   **
601 Klein Street
Vicksburg, MS 39180
(800) 444-7421; (601) 636-7421

SOUTHEAST

Ramada Limited   G,S,T,NS,OB   *
4216 Washington Street
Vicksburg, MS 39180
(601) 638-5750

NORTH CAROLINA

Albemarle
Comfort Inn   G,H,R,T   *
735 SR 24/27 Bypass
Albemarle, NC 28001
(704) 983-6990

Asheville
Econo Lodge   G,H,R,T   *
190 Tunnel Rd.
Asheville, NC 28805
(704) 254-9521

The Dogwood Cottage Inn   G,T,NS   **
40 Canterbury Rd.
Asheville, NC 28801
(704) 258-9725

Burlington
Comfort Inn   H,T   *
978 Plantation Dr.
Burlington, NC 27215
(910) 227-3681

Charlotte
Charlotte Hilton   N/A   **
8629 J. M. Keynes Dr.
Charlotte, NC 28262
(704) 547-7444

Comfort Inn   G,H,R   *
I-85 & Sugar Creek Rd.
Charlotte, NC 28269
(704) 598-0007

Days Inn   A,H,R,NS   *
118 East Woodlawn Road
Charlotte, NC 28217
(704) 525-5500

Marriott Residence Inn   S,SA   ***
8503 N. Tryon St.
Charlotte, NC 28262
(704) 547-1122

Concord
Days Inn   N/A   **
5125 Davidson Hwy.
I-85 & NC 73
Concord, NC 28027
(704) 786-9121

Dunn
Econo Lodge   G,R   *
513 Spring Branch Rd.
Dunn, NC 28334
(910) 892-6181

HoJo Inn   R,S,NS   *
510 Springbranch Rd.
I-95, Exit 72
Dunn, NC 28334
(910) 892-8711

Ramada Inn   G,H,R,S,T,NS   *
I-95 & US 421 Exit 73
PO Box 729
Dunn, NC 28334
(910) 892-8101

Durham
Marriott Residence Inn   A   ***
1919 Highway 54 East
Durham, NC 27713
(919) 361-1266

SOUTHEAST

Fayetteville
Comfort Inn   G,H,R   *
I-95 & SR 53
Fayetteville, NC 28302
(910) 323-8333

Rodeway Inn   G,R   *
2507 Gillespie St.
Fayetteville, NC 28306
(910) 485-5161

Greenville
Comfort Inn   H,R,T   *
Memorial Drive
Greenville, NC 27834
(800) 228-5150

Hickory
Econo Lodge   G,H,R,T   *
325 US 70 S.W.
Hickory, NC 28603
(704) 328-2111

HoJo Inn   R,S,NS   *
483 Highway 70 & 320 Sthwt
Hickory, NC 28603
(704) 322-1600

Kenly
Econo Lodge   H,R   *
US 301 & I-95
Kenly, NC 27542
(919) 284-1000

Kill Devil Hills
Ramada Inn Nags Head Beach   G,H,R,S,NS   *
1701 Virginia Dare Trail
Kill Devil Hills, NC 27948
(919) 441-2151

Marion
Scenic Inn   H,R   *
221 S. at I-40
Marion, NC 28752
(704) 659-7940

Salisbury
Econo Lodge   G,R,T   *
1011 E. Innes St.
Salisbury, NC 28144
(704) 633-8850

Rodeway Inn   G,H,R   **
321 Bendix Dr.
Salisbury, NC 28146
(704) 636-7065

Sleep Inn   G,H,R,T   *
321 Bendix Dr.
Salisbury, NC 28146
(704) 633-5961

Smithfield
Howard Johnson Lodge   H,R,S,NS   *
I-95 & US 70 Business
Smithfield, NC 27577
(919) 934-7176

Spruce Pine
Spruce Pine Motel   G,T,NS   **
423 Oak Avenue
Spruce Pine, NC 28777
(704) 765-9344

Statesville
Best Stay Inn   G,H,R,T   *
I-77 at exit 49B
Statesville, NC 28687
(704) 872-5215

SOUTHEAST

Tryon
The Foxtrot Inn   N/A   **
800 Lynn Road/Rt. 108
P.O. Box 1561
Tryon, NC 28782
(704) 859-9706

Williamston
Comfort Inn   H,R,T   *
US 64 Bypass
Williamston, NC 27892
(919) 792-8400

Wilson
Quality Inn   G,H,R   *
I-95 Bus Loop
Wilson, NC 27893
(919) 243-5165

Winston-Salem
Marriott Residence Inn   S,SA   ***
7835 North Point Blvd.
Winston-Salem, NC 27106
(910) 759-0777

SOUTH CAROLINA

Aiken
Ramada Limited   A,G,H,S,T,NS   *
1850 Richland Ave W.
Aiken, SC 29801
(803) 648-6821

Ramada Hotel   H,R,S,NS   *
Hwy 19 & I-20
Aiken, SC 29801
(803) 648-4272

Beaufort
Howard Johnson Lodge   H,R,S,NS   *
US Highway 21
Beaufort, SC 29902
(803) 524-6020

Bishopville
Econo Lodge   G,H,T   *
1153 S. Main St.
Bishopville, SC 29010
(803) 428-3200

Charleston
The Indigo Inn   N/A   **
1 Maiden Lane
Charleston, SC 29401
(803) 577-5900

Marriott Residence Inn   A   ***
7645 Northwoods Blvd.
North Charleston, SC 29406
(803) 572-5757

Middleton Inn   N/A   **
Ashley River Rd.
Charleston, SC 29407
(803) 556-0500

HoJo Inn   A,H,R,S,NS   *
3640 Dorchester Road
Charleston, SC 29405
(803) 554-4140

HoJo Inn   A,H,S,NS   *
2512 Ashley Phosphate Rd.
North Charleston, SC 29418
(803) 797-6864

SOUTHEAST

Columbia

HoJo Inn 200 Zimalcrest Road Columbia, SC 29210 (803) 772-7200	R,S,NS	*
HoJo Inn 494 Beltline Blvd. Columbia, SC 29205 (803) 738-1642	A,H,R,NS	*
Marriott Residence Inn 150 Stoneridge Drive Columbia, SC 29210 (803) 779-7000	A,G,P	***
Ramada Inn West 3 I-26 & US 378 West Columbia, SC 29169 (803) 796-2700	A,R,S,HS,NS	*

Dillon

Econo Lodge I-95 exit 193 Dillon, SC 29536 (803) 774-4181	R	*

Florence

Econo Lodge I-95 & US 52 Florence, SC 29502 (803) 665-8558	G,R,S,T	*
Howard Johnson I-95 & U.S. 76 Florence, SC 29506 (803) 664-9494	H,R,S,NS	*
Ramada Inn I-95 & US 52, Exit 164 Florence, SC 29501 (803) 669-4241	A,G,H,R,S,NS,SA	*

SOUTHEAST

Ft. Mill
Ramada Inn Carowinds 3   G,S,NS   *
225 Carowinds Blvd
Ft. Mill, SC 29715
(803) 548-2400

Greenville
Howard Johnson Lodge   A,R,S,T,NS   *
I-85 and Laurens Road
Greenville, SC 29607
(864) 288-6900

Marriott Residence Inn   A   **
48 McPrice Court
Greenville, SC 29615
(864) 297-0099

Ramada Hotel Downtown   G,R,S,T,NS   *
1001 S. Church St. at I-85
Greenville, SC 29601
(864) 232-7666

Greenwood
Econo Lodge   G,R,T   *
719 Bypass 25 NE
Greenwood, SC 29646
(803) 229-5329

Hardeeville
Howard Johnson Lodge   H,R,S,NS   *
PO Box 1107, I-95 and US 17
Hardeeville, SC 29927
(803) 784-2271

Hilton Head
Red Roof Inn   N/A   **
5 Regency Pkwy
Hilton Head, SC 29928
(803) 686-6808

Mt. Pleasant
Red Roof Inn   G,H,S,T,NS   *
301 Johnnie Dodds Blvd
Mt. Pleasant, SC 29464
(803) 884-1411

Richburg
Econo Lodge   G,H,T   *
Rt. 1, Box 182
Richburg, SC 29729
(803) 789-3000

Rock Hill
Rodeway Inn   H,R   **
656 Anderson Rd.
Rock Hill, SC 29730
(803) 329-2100

Howard Johnson Lodge   H,R,S,NS   *
2625 Cherry Road
Rock Hill, SC 29730
(803) 329-3121

Santee
Santee Resorts   R,S,T,NS   *
I-95 Exit 102 Road 400
PO Box 130
Santee, SC 29142
(803) 478-7676

Ramada Inn   G,H,R,S,NS   *
I-95 Exit 98 & Rt 6
Santee, SC 29142
(803) 854-2191

Spartanburg
Marriott Residence Inn   N/A   **
9011 Fairforest Road
Spartanburg, SC 29301
(864) 576-3333

Summerton
Econo Lodge   G,H,R   *
I-95 & SR 102
Summerton, SC 29148
(803) 485-2865

Sumter
Ramada Inn   G,H,R,S,NS   *
226 North Washington St
Sumter, SC 29151-0520
(803) 775-2323

TENNESSEE

Alcoa
Ramada Inn Knoxville   A,G,H,R,S,NS   *
Highway 129, PO Box 120
Alcoa, TN 37701
(615) 970-3060

Athens
Super 8   R,S,NS   *
I-75 & Hwy. 30 Exit 49
Athens, TN 37303
(423) 745-4500

Bristol
Econo Lodge   G,H,R   *
I-81 & US 11
Bristol, TN 37621
(423) 968-9119

Regency Inn   H,R,S,NS   *
975 Volunteer Parkway
Bristol, TN 37620
(423) 968-9474

Chattanooga
Comfort Inn   G,H,R,T   *
7717 Lee Hwy.
Chattanooga, TN 37421
(423) 894-5454

Econo Lodge   G,R   *
1417 St. Thomas St.
Chattanooga, TN 37412
(423) 894-1417

Guest House Inn   H,R,S,NS   *
100 West 21st Street
Chattanooga, TN 37408
(423) 265-3151

Ramada Inn   A,G,H,R,S,NS   *
I-75 South and US 41
Chattanooga, TN 37412
(423) 894-6110

Quality Inn   H,R,T   *
6710 Ringgold Rd.
Chattanooga, TN 37412
(423) 894-6820

Clarksville
Royal Inn   H,S,NS   *
3080 Guthrie Highway
Clarksville, TN 37040
(615) 648-8800

Ramada Inn   G,H,R,S,NS,SA   *
50 College St. PO Box 1222
Clarksville, TN 37041
(615) 552-3331

Quality Inn   H,R,S,SA   *
803 N. 2nd St.
Clarksville, TN 37040
(615) 645-9084

SOUTHEAST

Cleveland
Hospitality Inn G,H,S,T,NS *
I-75 at US 64 Bypass
PO Box 3896
Cleveland, TN 37320
(423) 479-4531

Columbia
Econo Lodge H,R *
SR 99 & I-65
Columbia, TN 38401
(615) 381-1410

Ramada Inn G,H,R,S,NS *
1208 Nashville Hwy
Columbia, TN 38401
(615) 388-2720

Cookeville
Howard Johnson Lodge H,R,S,NS *
2021 East Spring Street
Cookeville, TN 38501
(615) 526-3333

Cornersville
Econo Lodge H,R *
I-65 & SR 31
Cornersville, TN 37047
(615) 293-2111

Dickson
Knights Inn R,S,NS *
2328 Hwy 46 South
Dickson,TN 37055
(615) 446-3766

Dyersburg
Ramada Limited A,G,H,T,NS,SA *
2331 Lake Rd.
Dyersburg, TN 38024
(901) 287-0044

SOUTHEAST

Gatlinburg
Ramada Inn   G,H,R,T,NS,SA,SK,SW   *
756 Parkway
Gatlinburg, TN 37738
(423) 436-7881

Goodlettsville
Econo Lodge   G,H,R,T   *
320 Long Hollow Pike
Goodlettsville, TN 37072
(615) 859-4988

Hermitage
Ramada Limited 9   A,G,H,S,NS   *
I-40E & Old Hickory Blvd.
Hermitage, TN 37076
(615) 889-8940

Jackson
Best Western   A,G,H,S,NS   *
1849 Hwy 45 By-Pass & I-40
Jackson, TN 38305
(901) 668-4222

Jefferson City
Apple Valley Resort   N/A   **
1850 Paul Drive
Jefferson City, TN 37760
(800) 545-8160

Kingsport
Comfort Inn   H,R,SA   **
100 Indian Center Ct.
Kingsport, TN 37660
(615) 378-4418

Knoxville
Best Western   R,S,NS   *
118 Merchant Drive
Knoxville, TN 37912
(615) 688-3141

SOUTHEAST

Lebanon
Comfort Inn   G,H,R,SA   *
829 S. Cumberland St.
Lebanon, TN 37087
(615) 444-1001

Madison
Rodeway Inn   G,H,R,T   *
625 N. Gallatin Rd.
Madison, TN 37115
(615) 865-2323

Memphis
Comfort Inn   A,G,H,R,T   *
1581 Brooks Rd.
Memphis, TN 38116
(901) 345-3344

Howard Johnson Lodge   H,R,S,NS   *
1541 Sycamore View
Memphis, TN 38134
(901) 388-1300

Marriott Residence Inn   N/A   ***
6141 Old Poplar Pike
Memphis, TN 38119
(901) 685-9595

Brownestone Hotel   S,R   **
300 N. Second
Memphis, TN 38105
(901) 525-2511; (800) 468-3515

Comfort Inn Graceland   S,T,R   **
2411 Winchester Rd.
Memphis, TN 38116
(901) 332-2370; (800) 365-2370

SOUTHEAST

Milan
Ramada Limited   A,G,H,S,T,NS   *
U.S. Hwy 70/79 and 45
Milan, TN 38358
(901) 686-3345

Morristown
Ramada Inn   G,H,R,S,T,NS   *
I-81 & US 25 E, Exit 8
Morristown, TN 37815
(615) 587-2400

Murfreesboro
HoJo Inn   H,R,S,NS   *
2424 South Church Street
Murfreesboro, TN 37130
(615) 896-5522

Ramada Limited   A,G,H,S,T,NS   *
1855 South Church St.
Murfreesboro, TN 37130
(615) 896-5080

Nashville
Econo Lodge   G,H,R,T   *
2460 Music Valley Dr.
Nashville, TN 37214
(615) 889-0090

Econo Lodge   G,H,R,T   *
2403 Brick Church Pike
Nashville, TN 37207
(615) 226-9805

Comfort Inn   G,H,R,T   *
2306 Brick Church Pike
Nashville, TN 37207
(615) 226-9560

SOUTHEAST

Marriott Residence Inn　　　A,S,SA　　　　　　***
Maryland Farms
206 Ward Circle
Brentwood, TN 37027
(615) 371-0100

Pigeon Forge
Econo Lodge　　　　　　G,H,R,T,SK　　　　　**
2440 N. Parkway
Pigeon Forge, TN 37868
(615)428-1231

Holiday Inn Resort　　　　N/A　　　　　　　**
3230 Parkway
Pidgeon Forge,TN 37868
(800) HOLIDAY

Sweetwater
Comfort Inn　　　　　　G,R,T　　　　　　　*
803 S. Main St.
Sweetwater, TN 37874
(615) 337-6646

Quality Inn　　　　　　H,R,S　　　　　　　*
I-75 & SR 68
Sweetwater, TN 37874
(615) 337-3541

·MIDWEST

MIDWEST

MIDWEST

Illinois
Indiana
Kentucky
Michigan
Ohio
Wisconsin

Hotel Cost Codes (for average one-night stay)

*	$30-60/night
**	$61-100/night
***	$101-150/night
****	$151 and up/night
W	Hotel has weekly rates only

Note: costs may vary by season.

Hotel Amenity Codes

A	Airport nearby
H	Handicapped access
HS	Hair salon on premises
G	Golf within 10 miles
NS	Non-smoking rooms available
OB	Facility is on the beach
P	Playground on premises
R	Restaurant on premises
S	Swimming on premises
SA	Sauna on premises
SK	Skiing within 25 miles
T	Tennis within 10 miles

ILLINOIS

Alton
Comfort Inn   G,H,R,S,NS   *
1900 Homer M Adams Pkwy
Alton, IL 62002
(618) 463-0800

Bloomington
HoJo Inn   H,R,NS   *
401 Brock Drive
Bloomington, IL 61701
(309) 829-3100

Ramada Inn Bloomington   A,G,H,S,NS,SA   *
1219 Holiday Lane
Bloomington, IL 61704
(309) 662-5311

Ramada Inn West   A,G,A,T,NS,SA   *
403 Brock Dr.
Bloomington, IL 61701
(309) 829-7602

Champaign
Comfort Inn   G,H,R,S   *
305 Market View Dr.
Champaign, IL 61821
(217) 352-4055

Chicago
The Inn at University Village   G,H,R   ***
625 S. Ashland Ave.
Chicago, IL 60607
(312) 243-7200

The Essex Inn   N/A   ***
800 S. Michigan Ave.
Chicago, IL 60605
(312) 939-2800

Ramada Inn Lakeshore   N/A   ***
4900 S. Lakeshore Drive
Chicago, IL 60607
(312) 288-5800

Ambassador West   N/A   ***
1300 N. State Pkwy
Chicago, IL 60607
(312) 787-3700

Quality Inn   H,R   **
1 Midcity Plaza
Chicago, IL 60601
(312) 829-5000

Marriott Residence Inn   N/A   ***
201 East Walton
Chicago, IL 60611
(312) 943-9800

Danville
Comfort Inn   G,H,S   **
383 Lynch Dr.
Danville, IL 61832
(217) 443-8004

Ramada Inn   A,G,H,R,S,T,NS   *
I-74 & Lynch Road, Exit 220
Danville, IL 61832
(217) 446-2400

Deerfield
Marriott Residence Inn   N/A   ***
530 Lake Cook Rd.
Deerfield, IL 60015
(847) 940-4544

Downers Grove
Comfort Inn   G,H,R,T   **
3010 Finely Rd.
Downers Grove, IL 60515
(630) 515-1500

East Peoria
Best Western   G,H,R,S,NS   *
401 N. Main St.
East Peoria, IL 61611
(309) 699-7231

Effingham
Econo Lodge   H,S,SA   *
1205 N. Keller Dr.
Effingham, IL 62401
(217) 347-7131

Howard Johnson Lodge   A,H,R,NS   *
1606 W. Fayette Avenue
Effingham, IL 62401
(217) 342-4667

Ramada Inn   G,H,R,S,T,NS,SA   *
I-70/57 & Rte 32-33
Effingham, IL 62401
(217) 342-2131

Forsyth
Comfort Inn   G,H,R,S,T   *
134 Barnett Ave.
Forsyth, IL 62535
(217) 875-1166

Galesburg
Comfort Inn   G,H,R   *
907 W. Carl Sandburg Dr.
Galesburg, IL 61401
(309) 344-5445

Regency Hotel   H,R,S,NS   *
3282 N. Henderson
Galesburg, IL 61401
(309) 344-1111

MIDWEST

Ramada Inn   G,H,R,S,T,NS   *
29 Public Square
Galesburg, IL 61401
(309) 343-9161

Galena
Best Western Quiet House   R   **
9915 Hwy 20 East
Galena, IL 61036
(815) 777-2577

Triangle Motel   N/A   **
Highway 20
Galena, IL 61036
(815) 777-2897

Joliet
Comfort Inn   G,H,R,S,T   **
3235 Norman Ave.
Joliet, IL 60435
(815) 436-5141

Comfort Inn   G,H,R,S,T   **
135 S. Larkin Ave.
Joliet, IL 60436
(815) 744-1770

LaSalle
Peru Inn   A,H,R,S,NS   *
Route 251 and I-80
LaSalle, IL 61301
(815) 224-2500

Lincoln
Comfort Inn   G,H,R,S,T   *
2811 Woodlawn Rd.
Lincoln, IL 62656
(217) 725-3960

Lombard
Marriott Residence Inn	R	***

2001 S. Highland Ave.
Lombard, IL 60148
(630) 629-7800

Mattoon
Howard Johnson	A,R,S,NS	*

So. Rt 45 & I-57
Mattoon, IL 61938
(217) 235-4161

Moline
Comfort Inn	G,H,R,S,SK	**

2600 52nd Ave.
Moline, IL 61265
(309) 762-7000

Ramada Inn Quad City	A,G,H,R,S,NS	*

2620 Airport Rd
Moline, IL 61265
(309) 797-1211

Morris
Comfort Inn	G,H,S	*

70 Gore Rd.
Morris, IL 60450
(815) 942-1433

Mt. Vernon
Holiday Inn	A,G,H,R,S,T,NS,SA	*

I-57/64 at Illinois
222 Potomoc Blvd
Mt. Vernon, IL 63840
(618) 244-7100

Normal
Comfort Suites	G,H,R,S	**

310 Greenbriar Dr.
Normal, IL 61761
(309) 452-8588

MIDWEST

Palatine
Ramada Hotel 7   G,R,S,T,NS,SA   *
920 East Northwest Hwy
Palatine, IL 60067
(847) 359-6900

Pekin
Comfort Inn   G,H,R,S,SA   **
3240 N. Vandever Ave.
Pekin, IL 61554
(309) 353-4047

Peoria
Comfort Suites   G,H,R,S,T   **
4021 War Memorial
Peoria, IL 61614
(309) 688-3800

Pontiac
Comfort Inn   G,H,R,S,T   **
1821 W. Reynolds St.
Pontiac, IL 61764
(815) 842-2777

Quincy
Comfort Inn   G,H,R,S   *
4100 Broadway
Quincy, IL 62301
(217) 228-2700

Rockford
Comfort Inn   G,H,R,S   **
7392 Argus Dr.
Rockford, IL 61107
(815) 398-7061

Rosemont
Clarion Hotel   R,S,SA   **
6810-B N. Manheim Rd.
Rosemont, IL 60018
(847) 297-8464

MIDWEST

Quality Inn   R,S,SA   **
6810-A N. Manheim Rd.
Rosemont, IL 60018
(708) 297-1234

Schiller Park
Marriott Residence Inn   A,R   ***
9450 W. Lawrence Ave.
Schiller Park, IL 60176
(847) 725-2210

Springfield
Comfort Inn   G,H,R,S   **
3442 Freedom Dr.
Springfield, IL 62704
(217) 787-2250

Sleep Inn   G,H,R   *
3470 Freedom Dr.
Springfield, IL 62704
(217) 787-6200

Staunton
Super 8   A,G,H,T,NS   *
East Main Street
Staunton, IL 62088
(618) 635-5353

Campgrounds (All Accept Pets--only some are listed)
Arrowhead Acres/Clinton
Bail's Timberline Lake/ St. Elmo
Wonderland/ Galena
Palace/ Galena
Benton KOA/ Benton
Camp Hauberg/ Port Byron
Camp Sycamore/ Sycamore
Crooked Tree/ Millbrook
Egyptian Hills Marina/ Creal Springs
Fox Valley/ Crystal Lake
Hayman's Shady Oak/ New Douglas
La Salle-Peru KOA/ North Utica
Waupecan Valley Park/ Morris

MIDWEST

INDIANA

Anderson
Comfort Inn   G,H,R,S,T   *
2205 E. 59th St.
Anderson, IN 46013
(317) 644-4422

Bloomington
Clarion Inn   G,H,R,T,SK   **
9301 Fairfax Rd.
Bloomington, IN 47408
(812) 824-9904

Best Western   G,R,SK   **
4501 E. Third St.
Bloomington, IN 47401
(812) 332-2141

Brazil
Howard Johnson Lodge   A,H,R,NS   *
R.R. 14, Box 579
Brazil, IN 47834
(812) 446-2345

Elkhart
Econo Lodge   H,R   *
3440 Cassopolis St.
Elkhart, IN 46514
(219) 262-0540

Quality Hotel   H.R,S   **
300 S. Main St.
Elkhart, IN 46516
(219) 295-0280

Evansville
Comfort Inn   H,R,S   **
5006 E. Morgan Ave.
Evansville, IN 47715
(812) 477-2211

Blue Sky Inn   A,R,S,NS   *
2508 Business 41 North
Evansville, IN 47711
(812) 425-1092

Fishers
Ramada Limited-Northeast 5   A,G,R,S,T,NS   *
9780 North by Northeast Bvd.
Fishers, IN 46038
(317) 578-9000

Ft. Wayne
Comfort Suites   G,H,R,S   **
2908 Goshen Rd.
Ft. Wayne, IN 46802
(219)484-6262

Marriott Residence Inn   N/A   ***
4919 Lima Rd.
Ft. Wayne, IN 46808
(219) 484-4700

Greenwood
Comfort Inn   G,H,R,T   **
110 Sheek Rd.
Greenwood, IN 46143
(317) 887-1515

Hammond
Amerihost Inn   G,R,S,NS   *
7813 Indianapolis Blvd.
Hammond, IN 46324
(219) 845-4678

Indianapolis
Comfort Inn   G,H,R,S   **
8190 Summithill Dr.
Indianapolis, IN 46250
(317) 595-0700

MIDWEST

Comfort Inn   G,H,R,S,T   **
3880 W. 92nd St.
Indianapolis, IN 46268
(317) 872-3100

Econo Lodge   G,R   **
4505 S. Harding St.
Indianapolis, IN 46217
(317) 788-9361

HoJo Inn   H,R,S,NS   *
7050 E. 21st Street
Indianapolis, IN 46219
(317) 352-0481

HoJo Inn
2602 North High School Rd   A,R,S,NS   *
Indianapolis, IN 46224
(317) 291-8800

Ramada Inn South 1   A,G,H,R,S,NS   *
4514 South Emerson Ave
Indianapolis, IN 46203
(317) 787-3344

Ramada Hotel   A,G,H,R,S,T,NS   **
2500 S. High School Road
Indianapolis, IN 46241
(317) 244-3361

Quality Inn   G,H,R,T   **
8275 Craig St.
Indianapolis, IN 46250
(317) 841-9700

Marriott Residence Inn   S,SA   ***
5224 West Southern Ave.
Indianapolis, IN 46241
(317) 244-1500

Marriott Residence Inn   S   ***
350 West New York St.
Indianapolis, IN 46204
(800) 331-3131

Marriott Residence Inn   S,SA   ***
9765 Crosspoint Blvd..
Indianapolis, IN 46256
(317) 842-1111

Kokomo
Comfort Inn   G,H,R,S,T   *
522 Essex Dr.
Kokomo, IN 46901
(317) 452-5050

Lafayette
Comfort Suites   G,H,R,S   **
31 Frontage Rd.
Lafayette, IN 47905
(317) 447-0016

Radisson Hotel   R,S,NS   **
4343 State Road 26 East
Lafayette, IN 47095
(317) 447-0575

Marion
Comfort Suites   G,H,R   **
1345 N. Baldwin Ave.
Marion, IN 46952
(317) 651-1006

Merrillville
Marriott Residence Inn   S,SA,R   ***
8018 Delaware Place
Merrillville, IN 46268
(219) 791-9000

MIDWEST

Muncie
Comfort Inn   G,H,R,S   **
4011 W. Bethel
Muncie, IN 47304
(317) 282-6666

Richmond
Comfort Inn   H,R,S   *
912 Mendelson Dr.
Richmond, IN 47374
(317) 935-4766

Howard Johnson Lodge   R,S,NS   *
2525 Chester Blvd.
Richmond, IN 47374
(317) 962-7576

South Bend
Econo Lodge   H,R   **
3233 Lincoln Way W.
South Bend, IN 46628
(219) 232-9019

Taylorsville
Comfort Inn   G,H,R,T   **
10330 N. US 31
Taylorsville, IN 47280
(812) 526-9747

Terre Haute
Comfort Suites   G,H,R,T   **
501 E. Margaret Ave.
Terre Haute, IN 47802
(812) 235-1770

Warsaw
Comfort Inn   G,H,R   **
2605 E. Center St.
Warsaw, IN 46580
(219) 267-7337

MIDWEST

KENTUCKY

Bardstown
Ramada Inn G,H,S,T,NS *
523 North Third Street
Bardstown, KY 40004
(502) 349-0363

Berea
Econo Lodge G,H,R,T *
1010 Paint Lick Rd.
Berea, KY 40403
(606) 986-9323

Howard Johnson Lodge H,R,NS *
715 Chestnut St.
Berea, KY 40403
(606) 986-2384

Bowling Green
Ramada Inn G,H,R,S,NS *
4767 Scottsville Road
Bowling Green, KY 42104
(502) 781-3000

Cave City
Comfort Inn G,H,R *
I-65 exit 53
Cave City, KY 42127
(800) 228-5150

Quality Inn G,H,R *
Mammoth Cave Rd.
Cave City, KY 42127
(502) 773-2181

Clarksville
Econo Lodge G,H,R,T *
460 Auburn Ave.
Clarksville, KY 47129
(812) 288-6661

Covington
The Carneal Inn   N/A   **
405 East Second St.
Covington, KY 41011
(606) 431-6130; (606) 581-6041

Elizabethtown
Comfort Inn   H,R,S   **
1043 Executive Dr.
Elizabehtown, KY 42701
(502) 769-3030

Commonwealth Lodge   H,R,S,NS   *
708 East Dixie Avenue
Elizabethtown, KY 42701
(502) 765-2185

Franklin
Comfort Inn   G,H,R   *
Nashville Rd.
Franklin, KY 42134
(502) 586-6100

Fulton
Quality Inn   G,G,R,T   *
US 51 & Purchase Pkwy.
Fulton, KY 42041
(502) 472-2342

Gilbertville
Ramada Inn Resort   A,G,H,S,NS   *
Hwy 62, Box 158
Gilbertville, KY 42044
(502) 362-4278

Georgetown
Econo Lodge   G,R   *
3075 Paris Pike
Georgetown, KY 40324
(502) 863-2240

MIDWEST

Motel 6   G,H,S,T,NS   *
401 Delaplain, Box 926
Georgetown, KY 40324
(502) 863-1166

Hopkinsville
Econo Lodge   G,H,R,S   *
2916 Ft. Campbell Blvd.
Hopkinsville, KY 42240
(502) 886-5242

Rodeway Inn   G,R   *
2923 Ft. Campbell Blvd.
Hopkinsville, KY 42240
(502) 885-1126

Lexington
Econo Lodge   G,R,T   *
925 Newtown Pike
Lexington, KY 40511
(606) 231-6300

Econo Lodge   G,H,R   *
5527 Athens-Boonesboro Rd.
Lexington, KY 40509
(606) 263-5101

Quality Inn   G,R,T   *
1050 Newtown Pike
Lexington, KY 40511
(606) 233-0561

Days Inn South   R   ***
5575 Athens Boonesboro Rd.
Lexington, KY 40509
(606) 263-3100

Marriott's Griffin Gate   R   ***
1800 Newtown Pike
Lexington, KY 40509
(606) 231-5100

MIDWEST

Marriott Residence Inn   N/A   ***
1080 Newtown Pike
Lexington, KY 40511
(606) 231-6191

London
Ramada Inn   A,G,S,NS   *
2035 W 192 Bypass
London, KY 40741
(606) 864-7331

Louisville
Ramada Hotel Airport East 1   A,G,H,S,T,NS   *
1921 Bishop Lane
Louisville, KY 40218
(502) 456-4411

Quality Inn   R   **
3315 Bardstown Rd.
Louisville, KY 40218
(502) 452-1501

Marriott Residence Inn   N/A   ***
120 N. Hurstbourne Pkwy.
Louisville, KY 40222
(502) 425-1821

Mt. Vernon
Econo Lodge   G,R,T   *
I-75 & US 25
Mt. Vernon, KY 40456
(606) 256-4621

Murray
The Diuguid House   N/A   **
603 Main Street
Murray, KY 42071
(502) 753-5470

MIDWEST

Murray Plaza Court   N/A   **
P.O. Box 239
Murray, KY 42071
(502) 753-2682

Paducah
Quality Inn   G,H,R,T   *
1380 S. Irvin Cobb Dr.
Paducah, KY 42001
(502) 433-8751

Radcliff
Econo Lodge   G,R   *
261 N. Dixie Hwy.
Radcliff, KY 40160
(502) 351-4488

Richmond
Econo Lodge   G,R   *
230 Eastern Bypass
Richmond, KY 40475
(606) 623-8813

HoJo Inn   R,S,NS   *
1683 Northgate Drive
Richmond, KY 40475-1066
(606) 624-2612

MICHIGAN

Ann Arbor
Marriott Residence Inn   N/A   ***
800 Victors Way
Ann Arbor, MI 48108
(313) 996-5666

Comfort Inn   G,H,R,S,T,SK   **
2455 Carpenter Rd.
Ann Arbor, MI 48108
(313) 973-6100

MIDWEST

Lampost Inn   H,R,NS   *
2424 E. Stadium Blvd.
Ann Arbor, MI 48104
(313) 971-8000

Battle Creek
Holiday Inn   H,S,NS   *
2590 Capital Avenue SW
Battle Creek, MI 49015
(616) 965-3201

Benton Harbor
Comfort Inn   G,H,R,S   *
1598 Mall Dr.
Benton Harbor, MI 49022
(616) 925-1880

Ramada Inn   G,H,S,NS   *
798 Ferguson Dr
Benton Harbor, MI 49022
(616) 927-1172

Canton
Country Hearth   A,G,H,S,T,NS   *
40500 Michigan Avenue
Canton, MI 48188
(313) 721-5200

Cedarville
Comfort Inn   G,H,R,S,SA   **
210 W. SR 134
Cedarville, MI 49719
(906) 484-2266

Coldwater
Econo Lodge   G,R,T   *
884 W. Chicago Rd.
Coldwater, MI 49036
(517) 278-4501

Quality Inn 1000 Orleans Blvd. Coldwater, MI 49036 (517) 278-2017	H,R,S	**

Detroit

Ramada Hotel 400 Bagley Avenue Detroit, MI 48226 (313) 962-2300	A,H,R,S,NS	*
The Westin Hotel Renaissance Center Detroit, MI 48243 (313) 568-8000	R,S,NS,H	****
The Suburban House 16920 Telegraph Detroit, MI 48219 (313) 535-9646	S	**
Marriott Residence Inn 5777 Southfield Service Drive Detroit, MI 48228 (313) 441-1700	S,SA	***

Grand Rapids

Econo Lodge 250 28th St. Grand Rapids, MI 49548 (616) 452-2131	G,H,R,SK	*
Knights Inn 35-28th Street SW Grand Rapids, MI 49508 (616) 452-5141	H,R,S,NS	*
Marriott Residence Inn 2701 E. Beltline SE Grand Rapids, MI 49546 (616) 957-8111	A	***

MIDWEST

Hazel Park
Quality Inn   H,R   *
1 W. Nine Mile Rd.
Hazel Park, MI 48030
(810) 399-5800

Holland
Holland Fairfield Inn   S,NS,H   **
2854 W. Shore Drive
Holland, MI 49424
(800) 228-2800

Knights Court   S,NS,H   **
422 E. 32nd St.
Holland, MI 49423
(800) 843-5644

Jackson
Rodeway Inn   G,R   *
901 Rosehill Dr.
Jackson, MI 49202
(517) 787-1111

Kalamazoo
Clarion Hotel   A,H,R,S,NS,SA   *
3600 East Cork Street
Kalamazoo, MI 49001
(616) 385-3922

Lansing
Quality Suites   G,H,R,SA   **
3121 E. Grand River Rd.
Lansing, MI 48917
(517) 351-1440

Marriott Residence Inn   S,SA   ***
1600 E. Grand River Rd.
East Lansing, MI 48823
(517) 332-7711

Ludington
Lands Inn   G,H,R,S,T,NS,SA   *
4079 West US 10 at Brye Rd
Ludington, MI 49431
(616) 845-7311

Mackinaw City
Econo Lodge   G,R,T,SK   **
412 Nicolet St.
Mackinaw City, MI 49701
(616) 436-5026

Ramada Inn   G,H,R,S,NS,SA,SK   *
450 S Nicolet
Mackinaw City, MI 49701
(616) 436-5535

Kewadin Inn   R,SK   *
619 S. Nicolet St.
Mackinaw City, MI 49701
(616) 436-5332

Quality Inn   G,R,S,SA   **
917 S. Huron Dr.
Mackinaw City, MI 49701
(616) 436-5051

Manistique
Econo Lodge   G,H,R,T   *
E. Lakeshore Dr.
Manistique, MI 49854
(906) 341-6014

HoJo Inn   H,NS   *
726 East Lake Shore Drive
Manistique, MI 49854
(906) 341-6981

Kewadin Inn   A,H,R,S,NS,SA   *
US 2 E Lakeshore Dr
Manistique, MI 49854
(906) 341-6911

MIDWEST

Marquette
Ramada Inn A,G,R,S,NS,SA,SK **
412 W Washington Street
Marquette, MI 49855
(906) 228-6000

Menominee
HoJo Inn A,H,R,NS,OB *
2516 10th St.
Menominee, MI 49858
(906) 863-8802

Midland
Ramada Inn G,R,S,HS,NS *
1815 S. Saginaw Rd.
Midland, MI 48640
(517) 631-0570

Munising
Comfort Inn G,H,S *
SR 28 (M-28) E.
Munising, MI 49862
(906) 387-5292

New Buffalo
Comfort Inn G,H,R **
11539 O'Brien Ct.
New Buffalo, MI 49117
(616) 469-4440

Petoskey
Comfort Inn G,H,R,T,SK **
1314 US 31 N.
Petoskey, MI 49770
(616) 347-3220

Econo Lodge G,H,R,S,SK *
1858 US 131 S.
Petoskey, MI 49770
(616) 348-3324

Rochester
Howard Johnson Lodge   R,S,NS   *
111 SW 17th Avenue
Rochester, MI 55902
(507) 289-1617

Romulus
Days Inn   G,H,R   *
9501 Middlebelt Rd.
Romulus, MI 48174
(313) 946-4300

Saginaw
Comfort Suites   R,T   *
Fashion Sq.
Saginaw, MI 48601
(800) 228-5150

Southfield
Econo Lodge   G,R,SA   *
23300 Telegraph Rd.
Southfield, MI 48034
(810) 358-1800

Marriott Residence Inn   N/A   ***
26700 Central Park Blvd.
Southfield, MI 48076
(810) 352-8900

South Haven
Econo Lodge   R,S,T,SA,SK   **
09817 SR 140
South Haven, MI 49090
(616) 637-5141

St. Ignace
Howard Johnson Lodge   H,R,S,NS   *
913 Boulevard Drive
St. Ignace, MI 49781
(906) 643-9700

Traverse City
Rodeway Inn   G,R,SK   *
1582 US 31 N.
Traverse City, MI 48686
(616) 938-2080

Troy
Marriott Residence Inn   N/A   ***
2600 Livernois Rd.
Troy, MI 48083
(810) 689-6856

Warren
Marriott Residence Inn   N/A   ***
30120 Civic Center Blvd.
Warren, MI 48093
(810) 558-8050

OHIO

Akron
Marriott Residence Inn   N/A   ***
120 Montrose West Ave.
Akron, OH 44321
(330) 666-4811

Blue Ash
Marriott Residence Inn   G   ***
11401 Reed Hartman Hwy.
Blue Ash, OH 45241
(513) 530-5060

Bluffton
HoJo Inn   H,R,NS   *
855 St. Route 103
Bluffton, OH 45817
(419) 358-7000

Chillicothe
Comfort Inn   G,H,R,T   **
20 N. Plaza Blvd.
Chillicothe, OH 45601
(614) 775-3500

Cincinnati
Woodfield Suites   G,H,R,S,NS,SA   *
11029 Dowlin Drive
Cincinnati, OH 45241-1895
(513) 771-0300

Marriott Residence Inn S,SA   ***
11689 Chester Rd.
Cinncinnati, OH 45246
(513) 771-2525

Cleveland
Ramada Inn Cleveland G,H,S,T,NS   **
24801 Rockside Road
Cleveland, OH 44146
(216) 439-2500

Marriott Residence Inn N/A   ***
30100 Clemens Road
Cleveland, OH 44145
(216) 892-2254

Columbus
Econo Lodge   H,R,S,NS   *
5950 Scarborough Blvd
Columbus, OH 43232
(614) 864-4670

Quality Inn   G,H,R,T   **
4801 E. Broad St.
Columbus, OH 43213
(614) 861-0321

MIDWEST

Marriott Residence Inn   N/A   ***
2084 S. Hamilton Rd.
Columbus, OH 43232
(614) 864-8844

Curtice
Econo Lodge   H,R   *
10530 Corduroy Rd.
Curtice, OH 43412
(419) 836-2822

Dayton
Comfort Inn   G,H,R,S   *
7125 Miller Ln.
Dayton, OH 45414
(513) 890-9995

Ramada Inn North Airport   A,H,R,S,NS   *
4079 Little York Road
Dayton, OH 45414
(513) 890-9500

Howard Johnson   G,H,R   *
7575 Poe Ave.
Dayton, OH 45414
(513) 454-0550

Eaton
Econo Lodge   G,R,T   *
I-70 & US 127
Eaton, OH 45320
(513) 456-5959

Elyria
Comfort Inn   G,H,R,T   **
739 Leona St.
Elyria, OH 44035
(216) 324-7676

Erlanger
Comfort Inn   G,H,R   *
630 Donaldson Rd.
Erlanger, OH 41018
(606) 727-3400

Findlay
Econo Lodge   G,R   *
316 Emma St.
Findlay, OH 45840
(419) 422-0154

Jackson
Comfort Inn   G,H,R   **
605 E. Main St.
Jackson, OH 45640
(614) 286-7581

Kings Island
Holiday Inn   G,R   **
5589 Kings Mills Rd.
Kings Island, OH 45034
(513) 398-8075

Mansfield
Comfort Inn   H,R,S,SK   **
500 N. Trimble Rd.
Mansfield, OH 44906
(419) 529-1000

Econo Lodge   G,R,SK   *
1017 Koogle Rd.
Mansfield, OH 44903
(419) 589-3333

Marietta
Econo Lodge   G,H,R,T   *
702 Pike St.
Marietta, OH 45750
(614) 374-8481

MIDWEST

Marion
Comfort Inn	G,H,R,S,T	*
256 Jamesway		
Marion, OH 43302		
(614) 389-5552		

Ramada Inn	A,G,S,T,NS	*
1065 Delaware Avenue		
Marion, OH 43302		
(614) 383-6771		

Miamisburg
Marriott Residence Inn	N/A	***
155 Prestige Pl.		
Miamisburg, OH 45352		
(937) 434-7881		

Nelsonville
Quality Inn	H,R,S	*
US 33 & SR 691		
Nelsonville, OH 45764		
(614) 753-3531		

Perrysburg
Howard Johnson Lodge	H,R,S,NS	*
I-280 & Hanley Road		
Perrysburg, OH 43551		
(419) 837-5245		

Reynoldsburg
Northwestern Hotel	A,G,R,S,NS	*
2100 Brice Road		
Reynoldsburg, OH 43068		
(614) 864-1280		

Sandusky
Comfort Inn	H,R	**
1711 Cleveland Rd.		
Sandusky, OH 44870		
(419) 625-4700		

MIDWEST

Rodeway Inn   G,R,T   *
2905 Milan Rd.
Sandusky, OH 44870
(419) 625-1291

Seville
HoJo Inn   R,NS   *
I-71 & I-76
Seville, OH 44273
(330) 769-2053

Toledo
Clarion Inn   G,H,R,S,T   **
3536 Secor Rd.
Toledo, OH 43606
(419) 535-7070

Holiday Inn   A,G,S,T,HS,NS   **
2340 S. Reynolds Road
Toledo, OH 43614
(419) 865-1361

Vandalia
Park Inn   A,H,R,S,NS   *
75 Corporate Center Dr.
Vandalia, OH 45377
(513) 898-8321

Wooster
Econo Lodge   H,R,S   *
2137 Lincoln Way E.
Wooster, OH 44691
(330) 264-8883

Youngstown
Marriott Residence Inn   A,S,SA   ***
7396 Tiffany South
Poland, OH 44514
(330) 726-1747

MIDWEST

Campgrounds (Pet-friendly)
There are abut 140 campgrounds; more than half are pet friendly.
Selected ones are listed below.

Airport RV Park/Hebron
Audubon Lakes Campground/Geneva
Bass Lake Family Recreation/Springfield
Bay Shore/Andover
Camp America/Oxford
Camp Toodik/Loudonville
Charlie's Place/Lisbon
Dayton Tall Timbers KOA/Dayton
E-Z Camp Area/Wapakoneta
Foxfire Family Campground/Nevada
Honey-Do Campground/Spencer
Lazy R/Granville
Top 'O The Caves/Logan
Yogi Bear's Jellystone Park/Cinncinnati

WISCONSIN

Appleton
Comfort Suites   H,R,S,SA   **
3809 W. Wisconsin Ave.
Appleton, WI 54915
(414) 730-3800

Marriott Residence Inn   N/A   **
310 Metro Drive
Appleton, WI 54915
(414) 954-0570

Baraboo
HoJo Inn   A,H,R,S,NS   *
750 W. Pine
Baraboo, WI 53913
(608) 356-8366

Green Bay
Comfort Inn G,H,R,S,T **
2841 Ramada Way
Green Bay, WI 54304
(414) 498-2060

Marriott Residence Inn A,S,SA ***
335 W. St. Joseph St.
Green Bay, WI 54301
(414) 435-2222

Kenosha
Budgetel Inn N/A **
7540 118th Ave.
Kenosha, WI 53142
(414) 857-7911

Holiday Inn N/A **
5125 6th Ave.
Kenosha, WI 53140
(414) 658-3281

Madison
Ramada Limited A,G,S,T,NS,SK *
3841 E Washington Ave
Madison, WI 53704
(608) 244-2481

Marriott Residence Inn A,S,SA **
4862 Hayes Rd.
Madison, WI 53704
(608) 244-5047

Milwaukee
Howard Johnson Lodge A,R,S,NS *
1716 West Layton Avenue
Milwaukee, WI 53221
(414) 282-7000

Ramada Inn South Airport   A,G,R,S,T,NS,SA,SK   *
6401 S 13th Street
Milwaukee, WI 53221
(414) 764-5300

Marriott Residence Inn   A,S,SA   ***
7275 N. Port Washington Rd.
Glendale, WI 53217
(414) 352-0070

Montreal
Mt. Retreat Chalet   N/A   ***
White Cap Mt., P.O. Box D
Montreal, WI 54550
(715) 561-2776

Oshkosh
Howard Johnson Lodge   A,H,R,S,NS   *
1919 Omro Road
Oshkosh, WI 54901
(414) 233-1200

Sheboygan
Ramada Inn Harbor Cntr   G,H,R,NS   *
723 Center Ave
Sheboygan, WI 53081
(414) 458-1400

Tomah
Econo Lodge   G,H,R,S   *
2005 N. Superior
Tomah, WI 54660
(608) 372-9100

HoJo Inn   A,H,R,NS   *
I-90 & Hwy 131 (Exit 41)
Tomah, WI 54660
(608) 372-4500

Camping Information
(608) 266-2181

MIDWEST

SOUTH-
CENTRAL

SOUTH-CENTRAL

Arkansas
Kansas
Louisiana
Missouri
Oklahoma
Texas

Hotel Cost Codes (for average one-night stay)

*	$30-60/night
**	$61-100/night
***	$101-150/night
****	$151 and up/night
W	Hotel has weekly rates only

Note: costs may vary by season.

Hotel Amenity Codes

A	Airport nearby
H	Handicapped access
HS	Hair salon on premises
G	Golf within 10 miles
NS	Non-smoking rooms available
OB	Facility is on the beach
P	Playground on premises
R	Restaurant on premises
S	Swimming on premises
SA	Sauna on premises
SK	Skiing within 25 miles
T	Tennis within 10 miles

SOUTH-CENTRAL

ARKANSAS

Arkadelphia
Quality Inn   G,R   *
I-30 & SR 7
Arkadelphia, AR 71923
(501) 246-5855

Blytheville
Comfort Inn   G   *
I-55 & SR 18 E.
Blytheville, AR 72315
(501) 763-7081

Conway
Comfort Inn   H,R   *
150 US 65 N.
Conway, AR 72032
(501) 329-0300

Ramada Inn   S,A,H,T,R,P,NS   *
I-40 & US 64
Conway, AR 72032
(501) 329-8392

Crossett
Lakewood Inn   S,H,G,T,P,NS   **
1400 Arkansas Hwy
Crossett, AR 71635
(501) 364-4101

El Dorado
Comfort Inn   G,H,R,T   **
2303 Junction City Rd.
El Dorado, AR 71730
(501) 863-6677

Fayetteville
Ramada Inn   S,A,G,T,NS   **
3901 N. College Ave.
Fayetteville, AR 72703
(501) 443-3431

Sleep Inn   G,H,R,S   **
720 Millsap Rd.
Fayetteville, AR 72703
(800) SLEEP INN

Fort Smith
Ramada Inn Airport   S,A,H,G,R,NS   *
5103 Towson Ave.
Fort Smith, AR 72901
(501) 646-2931

Harrison
Ramada Inn   S,A,G,T,P,NS   *
1222 N. Main St.
Harrison, AR 72601
(501) 741-7611

Helena
The Edwardian Inn   N/A   **
317 South Biscoe
Helena, AR 72342
(501) 338-9155

Hope
Quality Inn   G,H,R   *
I-30 & SR 29
Hope, AR 71801
(501) 777-0777

Hot Springs
Quality Inn   H,R   *
1125 E. Grand Ave.
Hot Springs, AR 71901
(501) 624-3321

SOUTH-CENTRAL

Jonesboro
Ramada Limited   S,A,H,G,T,NS   *
3000 Apache Drive
Jonesboro, AR 72401
(501) 932-5757

Little Rock
Comfort Inn   G,H,R,T   *
3200 Bankhead Dr.
Little Rock, AR 72206
(501) 490-2010

Ramada Limited 2   S,A,H,G,T,NS   *
9709 I-30
Little Rock, AR 72209
(501) 568-6800

Memphis
Ramada Inn I-40 W-3   G,H,R,S,NS   *
210 I-40 West
Memphis, AR 72301
(501) 735-3232

Prescott
Comfort Inn   G,H,R,T   *
SR 24 W., Rt. 5
Prescott, AR 71857
(501) 887-6641

KANSAS

Atchison
Comfort Inn   G,H,R,SK   *
405 S. 9th St.
Atchison, KS 66002
(913) 367-7666

SOUTH-CENTRAL

Colby
Comfort Inn   G,H,R,S   *
2225 S. Range
Colby, KS 67701
(913) 462-3833

Econo Lodge   G,H,R   *
1985 S. Range
Colby, KS 67701
(913) 462-8201

Ramada Inn   A,G,H,R,S,NS   *
1950 S Range
P.O. Box 487
Colby, KS 67701
(913) 462-3933

Dodge City
Econo Lodge   G,H,R,S,T,SA   *
1610 W. Wyatt Earp Blvd.
Dodge City, KS 67801
(316) 225-0231

Emporia
Comfort Inn   G,R,T   *
2511 W. 18th
Emporia, KS 66801
(316) 343-7750

Ramada Inn   A,G,H,R,S,T,NS   *
1839 Merchant
Emporia, KS 66801
(316) 342-8850

Quality Inn   G,R,S   *
3021 W. US 50
Emporia, KS 66801
(316) 342-3770

Hutchinson
Comfort Inn   G,H,R,SA   *
1621 Super Plaza
Hutchinson, KS 67501
(316) 663-7822

Ramada Inn   G,H,R,S,T,NS,SA   *
1400 North Lorraine
Hutchinson, KS 67501
(316) 669-9311

Quality Inn   G,H,R,T   *
15 W. 4th St.
Hutchinson, KS 67501
(316) 663-1211

Junction City
Econo Lodge   G,H,R   *
211 W. Flinthills Blvd.
Junction City, KS 66441
(913) 238-8181

Leavenworth
Ramada Inn   H,R,S,NS   *
101 So. 3rd St.
Leavenworth, KS 66048
(913) 651-5500

Ottawa
Econo Lodge   H,R,T   *
2331 South Cedar
Ottawa, KS 66067
(913) 242-3400

Overland Park
Marriott Residence Inn   N/A   **
6300 W. 110th
Overland Park, KS 66211
(913) 491-3333

SOUTH-CENTRAL

Salina
Comfort Inn   G,H,R,S,T   **
1820 W. Crawford St.
Salina, KS 67401
(913) 826-1711

Ramada Inn   H,R,S,NS   *
1949 N. 9th Street
Salina, KS 67401
(913) 825-8211

Topeka
Comfort Inn   G,H,R,S   **
1518 S.W. Wanamaker Rd.
Topeka, KS 66604
(913) 273-5365

Econo Lodge   G,H,R,S,T   *
1240 S.W. Wanamaker Rd.
Topeka, KS 66604
(913) 273-6969

Southtown Inn   A,G,R,S,T,NS   *
3847 S. Topeka Avenue
Topeka, KS 66609
(913) 267-1800

Wichita
Comfort Inn   G,H,R   *
4849 S.Laura
Wichita, KS 67216
(316) 522-1800

Marriott Residence Inn   N/A   **
411 S. Webb Rd.
Wichita, KS 67207
(316) 686-7331

Winfield
Comfort Inn   G,H,R   *
US 77 at Quail Ridge
Winfield, KS 67156
(316) 221-7529

LOUSIANA

Alexandria
Ramada Inn   A,G,H,R,S,NS   *
2211 North MacArthur Drive
Alexandria, LA 71301
(318) 443-2561

Rodeway Inn   G,R   *
742 MacArthur Dr.
Alexandria, LA 71301
(318) 448-1611

Baton Rouge
Comfort Inn   G,H   **
2445 S. Acadian Thruway
Baton Rouge, LA 70808
(504) 927-5790

Bossier
Ramada Inn   A,G,R,S,T,NS   *
150 Hamilton Rd.
Bossier, LA 71111
(318) 746-8410

Marriott Residence Inn   A,S,SA   **
1001 Gould Drive
Bossier City, LA 71111
(318) 747-6220

Chalmette
Quality Inn   H,R   **
5333 Paris Rd.
Chalmette, LA 70043
(504) 277-5353

Darrow
Texcuco Plantation   R   ***
3138 Hwy. 44
Darrow, LA 70725
(504) 562-3929

Houma
Quality Inn   G,R,T   **
1400 W. Tunnel Blvd.
Houma, LA 70360
(504) 879-4871

Lafayette
Comfort Inn   H,R   *
1421 S.E. Evangeline Thruway
Lafayette, LA 70501
(318) 232-9000

Rodeway Inn   H,R   *
1810 N.W. Evangeline Thruwy
Lafayette, LA 70501
(318) 233-5500

Metaire
Quality Inn   R,S,NS   *
2261 N. Causeway Blvd.
Metaire, LA 70001
(504) 833-8211

Monroe
Days Inn   A,H,R,S,NS   *
5650 Frontage Road
Monroe, LA 71202
(318) 345-2220

New Orleans
Prytania Inn   G,R,T   **
1415 Prytania St.
New Orleans, LA 70130
(504) 566-1515

SOUTH-CENTRAL

B&B at The Chimes   G,R,T   **
1360 Moss St., P.O. Box 52257
New Orleans, LA 70152-2257
(504) 488-4640

Glimmer Inn   G,R,T   **
1631 Seventh Street
New Orleans, LA 70115
(504) 897-1895

HoJo Inn   A,R,S,NS   *
4200 Old Gentilly Road
New Orleans, LA 70126
(504) 944-0151

Clarion Inn   G,R,T   **
501 Decatur St.
New Orleans, LA 70130
(504) 561-5621

New Orleans Hilton Riverside   A,S,SA,G,T   ***
2 Poydras St.
New Orleans, LA 70140
(504) 561-0500

Slidell
Comfort Inn   G,H,R,S   **
2010 Old Spanish Trail
Slidell, LA 70458
(504) 641-4147

Econo Lodge   G,H,R   **
I-10 & Gause Blvd.
Slidell, LA 70459
(504) 641-2153

Thibodaux
Howard Johnson Lodge   H,R,S,NS   *
201 North Canal Blvd.
PO Box 1144
Thibodaux, LA 70301
(504) 447-9071

SOUTH-CENTRAL

MISSOURI

Berkeley
Ramada Inn   G,R,SA   **
9600 Natural Bridge Rd.
Berkeley, MO 63134
(314) 427-7600

Blue Springs
Ramada Limited   G,S,NS   *
1100 N. 7 Highway
Blue Springs, MO 64014
(816) 229-6363

Branson
Quality Inn   G,H,R   *
3269 Shepherd Hills Expwy.
Branson, MO 65616
(417) 335-6776

Howard Johnson   H,R,S,NS   **
3027-A West Highway 76
Branson, MO 6566
(417) 336-5151

Bridgeton
Econo Lodge   G,R   *
4575 N. Lindbergh Blvd.
Bridgeton, MO 63044
(314) 731-3000

Columbia
Econo Lodge   G,H,S,T,SA   *
900 I-70 D., S.W.
Columbia, MO 65203
(314) 442-1191

HoJo Inn   R,S,NS   *
Exit 121, 6401 W. Hwy. 40
Columbia, MO 65202
(314) 445-9565

Ramada Inn   G,H,R,S,NS   *
1100 Vandiver Drive
Columbia, MO 65202
(314) 449-0051

Eureka
Ramada Inn   G,H,R,S,NS,SA   *
I-44 & Alentown Road
Eureka, MO 63025
(314) 938-6661

Hayti
Comfort Inn   G,H,R,T   *
I-55 & SR 84
Hayti, MO 63851
(314) 359-0023

Independence
Howard Johnson Lodge   H,R,S,NS   *
4200 South Noland Road
Independence, MO 64055
(816) 373-8856

Jefferson City
Ramada Inn   A,G,H,R,S,T,NS   *
1510 Jefferson
Jefferson City, MO 65109
(573) 635-7171

Kansas City
Benjamin Hotel & Suites   H,R,S,NS   **
6101 E 87th Street
Kansas City, MO 64138
(816) 765-4331

Marriott Residence Inn   N/A   ***
9900 NW Prairie View Rd.
Kansas City, MO 64153
(816) 891-9009

SOUTH-CENTRAL

Kearney
Econo Lodge   H,R   *
505 Shanks Ave.
Kearney, MO 64060
(816) 628-5111

Kirksville
Comfort Inn   G,H,R   *
2209 N. Baltimore
Kirksville, MO 63501
(816) 665-2205

Lansing
Econo Lodge   G,R,SK   *
504 N. Main St.
Lansing, MO 66043
(913) 727-2777

Lebanon
Econo Lodge   H,R   *
I-44 W. Bus Loop
Lebanon, MO 65536
(417) 588-3226

Lees Summit
Comfort Inn   H,R,S   *
607 S.E. Oldham Pkwy.
Lees Summit, MO 64063
(816) 524-8181

Merriam
Comfort Inn   H,R,T   *
6401 E. Frontage Rd.
Merriam, MO 66202
(913) 262-2622

Monroe City
Econo Lodge   G,H,R,S   *
3 Gateway Sq.
Monroe City, MO 63456
(314) 735-4200

SOUTH-CENTRAL

Oak Grove
Econo Lodge   G,R   *
410 S.E. 1st St.
Oak Grove, MO 64075
(816) 625-3681

O'Fallon
Comfort Inn   H,R   **
1100 Eastgate Dr.
O'Fallon, MO 62269
(618) 624-6060

Rolla
Econo Lodge   G,R,T   *
1417 Martin Spring Dr.
Rolla, MO 65401
(573) 341-3130

Howard Johnson Lodge   H,R,S,NS   *
127 NH Drive at I-44
Rolla, MO 65401
(573) 364-7111

Ramada Inn   G,H,R,S,T,NS   *
1701 Martin Spring Rd
Rolla, MO 65401
(573) 364-7977

Sikeston
Econo Lodge   R   *
110 S. Interstate, I-55
Sikeston, MO 63801
(573) 471-7400

Springfield
Comfort Inn   G,R,S,T   **
2550 N. Glenstone
Springfield, MO 65803
(417) 866-5255

SOUTH-CENTRAL

Travel Lodge   G,H,R,T   *
2610 N. Glenstone Ave.
Springfield, MO 65803
(417) 866-6671

St. Charles
Comfort Inn   G,H,R   *
2750 Plaza Way
St. Charles, MO 63303
(314) 949-8700

St. Genevieve
Family Budget   G,H,R   *
I-55 at Ozora Exit
St. Genevieve, MO 63670
(573) 543-2272

St. James
Comfort Inn   G,H,R,S   *
110 N. Outer Rd.
St. James, MO 65559
(314) 265-5005

St. Joseph
Ramada Inn   G,H,R,S,NS,SK   *
4016 Frederick Blvd.
St. Joseph, MO 64506
(816) 233-6192

St. Louis
Comfort Inn   G,H,R   **
12031 Lackland Rd.
St. Louis, MO 63146
(314) 878-1400

Comfort Inn   G,R   *
3730 S. Lindbergh Blvd.
St. Louis, MO 63127
(314) 842-1200

SOUTH-CENTRAL

Holiday Inn   H,R,NS   **
5915 Wilson Ave.
St. Louis, MO 63110
(314) 645-0700

Henry the 8th   A,G,H,R,S,NS,SA   *
4690 North Lindbergh
St. Louis, MO 63044
(314) 731-3040

Marriott Residence Inn   A.S.SA   **
1100 McMorrow Ave.
St. Louis, MO 63117
(314) 862-1900

St. Robert
Econo Lodge   G,H,R   *
I-44 & Ft. Leonard Wood
St. Robert, MO 65583
(573) 336-7272

Ramada Inn Ft. Wood   A,G,S,HS,NS   *
I-44 at Fort Wood Exit
St. Robert, MO 65583
(573) 336-3121

Warrenton
Motel 6   G   *
804 N. SR 47
Warrenton, MO 63383
(314) 456-2522

Wentzville
Ramada Limited   G,H,R   *
1400 Continental Dr.
Wentzville, MO 63385
(314) 327-5515

SOUTH-CENTRAL

West Plains
Ramada Inn   A,G,H,R,S,T,NS   *
1301 Preacher Roe Blvd
West Plains, MO 65775
(417) 256-8191

OKLAHOMA

Altus
Ramada Inn   A,G,H,R,S,T,NS   *
2515 E Broadway
Altus, OK 73521
(405) 477-3000

Ardmore
Comfort Inn   G,H,R   *
2700 W. Broadway
Ardmore, OK 73401
(405) 226-1250

Holiday Inn   N/A   **
2705 Holiday Dr.
Ardmore, OK 73401
(405) 223-7130   .

Blackwell
Comfort Inn   G,H,R,S   *
1201 N. 44th St.
Blackwell, OK 74631
(405) 363-7000

Broken Arrow
Econo Lodge   G,R,T   *
1401 N. Elm Pl.
Broken Arrow, OK 74012
(918) 258-6617

Chandler
Econo Lodge   G,H,R   *
600 N. Price
Chandler, OK 74834
(405) 258-2131

Elk City
Econo Lodge   G,R,T   *
108 Meadow Ridge
Elk City, OK 73644
(405) 225-5120

Knights Inn   R,NS   *
2604 E. Hwy 66
Elk City, OK 73644
(405) 225-2241

Enid
Econo Lodge   G,R,T   *
2523 Mercer Dr.
Enid, OK 73701
(405) 237-3090

Ramada Inn   A,G,H,R,S,T,NS   *
3005 W Garriott Road
Enid, OK 73703
(405) 234-0440

Erick
Comfort Inn   G,H,R,S,SA   *
I-40 Exit 7
Erick, OK 73645
(800) 228-5150

Lawton
Howard Johnson Hotel   A,R,S,NS   *
1125 E. Gore Blvd.
Lawton, OK 73501
(405) 353-0200

SOUTH-CENTRAL

Ramada Inn   A,G,H,R,S,T,NS   *
601 N 2nd
Lawton, OK 73507
(405) 355-7155

Holiday Inn   N/A   **
3134 Cache Rd.
Lawton, OK 73505
(405) 353-1682

Mcalester
Days Inn   N/A   **
Rt. 8 /Box 155
Mcalester, OK 74501
(918) 426-5050

Muskogee
Ramada Inn   G,H,R,S,NS,SA   *
800 S. 32nd St.
Muskogee, OK 74401
(918) 682-4341

Norman
Marriott Residence Inn   N/A   **
2681 Jefferson
Norman, OK 73072
(405) 366-0900

Oklahoma City
Econo Lodge   G,H,R   *
820 S. MacArthur Blvd.
Oklahoma City, OK 73128
(405) 947-8651

Howard Johnson Lodge   A,R,S,NS   *
400 South Meridian
Oklahoma City, OK 73108
(405) 943-9841

Ramada Limited   G,H,R,S,T,NS   *
1401 NE Expressway
Oklahoma City, OK 73111
(405) 478-5221

Pryor
Pryor House Motor Inn   N/A   **
123 S. Mill St.
Pryor, OK 74361
(918) 825-6677

Sallisaw
Econo Lodge   G,R   *
2403 E. Cherokee
Sallisaw, OK 74955
(918) 775-7981

Tulsa
Comfort Inn   G,H,R,T   *
4717 S. Yale Ave.
Tulsa, OK 74135
(918) 622-6776

Downtown Plaza Hotel   A,R,S,NS   *
17 W. 7th Street
Tulsa, OK 74119
(918) 585-5898

Ramada Hotel   G,R,S,HS,NS   *
5000 E. Skelly Dr
Tulsa, OK 74135
(918) 622-7000

Yukon
Comfort Inn   G,H,R,T   *
321 N. Mustang Rd.
Yukon, OK 73099
(405) 324-1000

SOUTH-CENTRAL

TEXAS

Abilene
Econo Lodge   R   *
1633 W. Stamford
Abilene, TX 79601
(915) 675-5424

Ramada Inn   A,G,H,R,S,NS   *
3450 S. Clack
Abilene, TX 79606
(915) 695-7700

Quality Inn   G,R,T   *
505 Pine St.
Abilene, TX 79601
(915) 676-0222

Alpine
The Corner House   G,R,T   **
801 E. Ave. E
Alpine, TX 79830
(915) 837-7161

Highland Inn   G,R,T   **
1404 E. Hwy 90
Alpine, TX 79830
(915) 837-5811

Amarillo
Comfort Inn   G,H,R   *
2100 S. Coulter Dr.
Amarillo, TX 79106
(806) 335-1561

Econo Lodge   G,H,R   *
I-40 & Lakeside Dr.
Amarillo, TX 79106
(806) 355-3321

Arlington

Ramada Inn   G,R,S,NS   *
700 E. Lamar Blvd
Arlington, TX 76011
(817) 265-7711

Marriott Residence Inn   N/A   **
1050 Brookhollow Plaza Dr.
Arlington, TX 76006
(817) 649-7300

Austin

Four Points Hotel   A,R,S   **
7800 North I-35
Austn, TX 78753
(512) 836-8520

Doubletree Guest Suites   S,R,T,G   ***
303 West 15th St.
Austin, TX 78701
(512) 478-7000

Rodeway Inn   G,R,T   *
5526 N. I-35
Austin, TX 78751
(512) 451-7001

Quality Inn   G,H,R,T   *
909 E. Koening Ln.
Austin, TX 78751
(512) 452-4200

Beaumont

Ramada Limited   G,H,R,T   *
4085 I-10 S.
Beaumont, TX 77705
(409) 842-9341

Quality Inn   G,H,R   *
1295 N. 11th St.
Beaumont, TX 77702
(409) 892-7722

SOUTH-CENTRAL

Belton
Ramada Limited   G,S,T,NS   *
1102 East 2nd by I-35
Belton, TX 76513
(817) 939-3745

Brownsville
Howard Johnson Hotel   H,R,S,NS   *
1945 North Expressway
Brownsville, TX 78520
(210) 546-4591

Brownwood
Best Western   G,H,R,SA   **
410 E. Commerce St.
Brownwood, TX 76801
(915) 646-3511

Burnet
HoJo Inn   R,S,NS   *
908 Buchanan Dr., Hwy 29 West
Burnet, TX 78611
(512) 756-4747

Childress
Comfort Inn   G,H,R,SA   *
1804 Ave. F N.W.
Childress, TX 79201
(817) 937-6363

Econo Lodge   G,R   *
1612 F N.W., US 287
Childress, TX 79201
(817) 937-3695

Clifton
The River's Bend B&B   N/A   **
P.O. Box 228
Clifton, TX 76634
(817) 675-4936

SOUTH-CENTRAL

College Station
Ramada Inn   A,G,H,R,S,T,NS   *
1502 Texas Ave
College Station, TX 77840
(409) 693-9891

Conroe
Ramada Limited   A,G,H,S,NS   *
1520 S. Frazier
Conroe, TX 77301
(409) 756-8939

Corpus Christi
Comfort Inn   R,SA   **
902 N. Navigation Blvd.
Corpus Christi, TX 78409
(800) 228-5150

Howard Johnson Marina Hotel   R,S,T,NS   **
300 N. Shoreline Blvd.
Corpus Christi, TX 78401
(512) 883-5111

Hampton Inn   A,H,R,S,T,NS,SA   *
5501 I-37
Corpus Christi, TX 78408
(512) 289-5861

Corsicana
Rodeway Inn   G,R   *
2021 Regal Dr.
Corsicana, TX 75110
(903) 874-4751

Dalhart
Friendship Inn   G,R,T   *
123 Liberal St.
Dalhart, TX 79022
(806) 249-6464

SOUTH-CENTRAL

Dallas
Howard Johnson   H,R,S,NS   **
9386 LBJ Fwy
Dallas, TX 75243
(214) 690-1220

Marriott Residence Inn   N/A   ***
6950 N. Stemmons Freeway
Dallas, TX 75247
(214) 631-2472

Ramada Hotel   A,G,R,S,T,NS   *
1011 South Akard
Dallas, TX 75215
(214) 421-1083

Ramada Hotel-Market Center 3 A,G,R,S,T,HS,NS   **
1055 Regal Row
Dallas, TX 75247
(214) 634-8550

Quality Suites   G,H,R   *
4700 John Carpenter Fwy.
Dallas, TX 75063
(800) 228-5150

Decatur
Comfort Inn   H,R,SA   *
1709 SR 287
Decatur, TX 76234
(817) 627-6919

Dumas
Econo Lodge   G,H,R,T   *
1719 S. Dumas Ave.
Dumas, TX 79029
(806) 935-9098

Eastland
Econo Lodge   G,H,R   *
2001 I-20 W.
Eastland, TX 76448
(817) 629-3324

El Paso
Comfort Inn   G,H,R   **
900 Yarbrough Dr.
El Paso, TX 79915
(915) 594-9111

Econo Lodge   G,R   *
6363 Montana Ave.
El Paso, TX 79925
(915) 778-3311

Howard Johnson Lodge   A,H,R,S,NS   *
8887 Gateway West
El Paso, TX 79925
(915) 591-9471

Fredericksburg
Comfort Inn   G,H,R,T   *
908 S. Adams St.
Fredericksburg, TX 78624
(210) 997-9811

Econo Lodge   H,R   *
810 S. Adams
Fredericksburg, TX 78624
(210) 997-3437

Ft. Stockton
Econo Lodge   G,H,R   *
800 E. Dickinson
Ft. Stockton, TX 79735
(915) 336-8531

SOUTH-CENTRAL

Ft. Worth
Marriott Residence Inn   N/A   ***
1701 S. University Drive
Fort Worth, TX 76107-6535
(817) 870-1011

Gainesville
Comfort Inn   G,H,R   *
1936 I-35 N.
Gainesville, TX 76240
(817) 665-5599

Georgetown
La Quinta Inn   G,H,R,S,T,NS   *
333 N I-35
Georgetown, TX 78628
(512) 869-2541

Hillsboro
Ramada Inn   G,H,R,S,NS   *
I-35 Hwy 22, PO Box 1205
Hillsboro, TX 76645
(817) 582-3493

Houston
Howard Johnson Lodge   A,R,S,NS   *
4225 North Freeway
Houston, TX 77022
(713) 695-6011

Holiday Inn   H,R,S,NS   *
7787 Katy Freeway
Houston,TX 77024
(713) 681-5000

Marriott Residence Inn   S,SA   **
525 Bay Area Blvd.
Houston, TX 77058
(281) 486-2424

SOUTH-CENTRAL

Ramada Plaza Northwest 3   G,H,S,T,NS,SA   **
12801 NW Freeway
Houston, TX 77040
(713) 462-9977

Ramada Inn South   G,R,S,NS   *
1301 NASA Road One
Houston, TX 77058
(713) 488-0220

Ramada Limited   G,H,S,T,NS   *
15725 Bammel Village Dr.
Houston, TX 77014
(713) 893-5666

Ramada Hotel   G,H,R,S,T,HS,NS   *
2100 S. Braeswood
Houston, TX 77030
(713) 797-9000

Quality Inn   G,H,R,T   **
6115 Will Clayton Pkwy.
Houston, TX 77205
(713) 446-9131

Jasper
Ramada Inn   G,H,R,S,T,NS   *
239 East Gibson
Jasper, TX 75951
(409) 384-9021

Kilgore
Ramada Inn Kilgore/Longview   A,G,H,R,S,NS   *
3501 Highway 259 N
Kilgore, TX 75662
(903) 983-3456

Lake Jackson
Ramada Inn   G,H,R,S,T,NS   **
925 Hwy. 332
Lake Jackson, TX 77566
(409) 297-1161

SOUTH-CENTRAL

La Rue
Dunsavage Farms   G,R,T   **
Box 176
La Rue, TX 75770
(800) 440-2959

Lewisville
Ramada Inn 9   A,G,H,R,S,NS   *
1102 Texas St
Lewisville, TX 75067
(214) 221-2121

Livingston
Ramada Inn   G,H,R,S,T,NS   *
1200 N. Washington
Livingston, TX 77351
(409) 327-3366

Longview
Ramada Limited   A,G,S,NS,SA   *
3304 S. Eastman Road
Longview, TX 75602
(903) 758-0711

Lubbock
Marriott Residence Inn   N/A   ***
2551 S. Loop 289
Lubbock, TX 79423
(806) 745-1963

McKinney
Comfort Inn   G,H,R,T   *
2104 N. Central Expwy.
McKinney, TX 75070
(214) 548-8888

Mineral Wells
HoJo Inn   S   *
2809 Hwy 180 West
Mineral Wells, TX 76067
(817) 328-1111

SOUTH-CENTRAL

Nacogdoches
Econo Lodge   G,H,R   *
2020 N.W. Loop 224
Nacogdoches, TX 75961
(409) 569-0880

New Braunfels
Rodeway Inn   G,H,R,T   *
1209 I-35 E.
New Braunfels, TX 78130
(210) 629-6991

Orange
Ramada Inn   G,H,R,S,NS   *
26101 I-10, E Bound 16 St
W. Bound Adams Bayou Exit,
Orange, TX 77630
(409) 883-0231

Palestine
Ramada Inn   G,H,R,S,T,NS   *
1101 E Palestine Ave, Hwy 79
Palestine, TX 75801
(903) 723-7300

Port Arthur
Ramada Inn   A,G,H,R,S,T,NS   *
3801 Hwy 73
Port Arthur, TX 77642
(409) 962-9858

Richardson
Clarion Hotel   G,H,R,S,SA   **
1981 N. Central Expwy.
Richardson, TX 75080
(214) 644-4000

Robstown
Econo Lodge   G,H,R   *
2225 US 77 N.
Robstown, TX 78380
(512) 387-9444

SOUTH-CENTRAL

Salado
HoJo Inn   R,S,NS   *
Rt. 2, Box 270-A
Salado, TX 76571
(817) 947-5000

San Antonio
Clarion Suites Hotel   G,H,R,T   **
13101 E. Loop 1604 N.
San Antonio, TX 78233
(210) 655-9491

Howard Johnson Lodge   A,R,S,NS   *
9603 IH-35 North
San Antonio, TX 78233
(210) 655-2120

Howard Johnson Lodge   A,H,R,S,NS   *
2755 IH-35 North
San Antonio, TX 78219
OPENING SOON

Marriott Residence Inn   A,S   **
425 Bonham St.
San Antonio, TX 78205
(210) 212-5555

Ramada Limited Northwest 3   A,H,S,NS   *
9447 I-10 West
San Antonio, TX 78230
(210) 558-9070

Sherman
Best Western   G,H,S,T,NS   *
2105 Texoma Parkway
Sherman, TX 75090
(903) 892-2161

Temple

Econo Lodge
1001 N. General Bruce Dr.
Temple, TX 76504
(817) 771-1688

G,H,R,T   *

HoJo Inn
1912 South 31st Street
Temple, TX 76504
(817) 778-5521

A,S,NS   *

Guest House Inn
400 SW Dodgen (Loop 363)
Temple, TX 76504
(817) 773-1515

A,G,H,S,T,NS   *

Texarkana

Comfort Inn
5105 Stateline Ave.
Texarkana, TX 75501
(903) 792-6688

G,H,R   *

Ramada Inn
I-30 at Summerhill Rd
Texarkana,TX 75501
(903) 794-3131

A,G,H,R,S,HS,NS   *

Tyler

Econo Lodge
3201 W. Gentry Pkwy.
Tyler, TX 75702
(903) 593-0103

G,R   *

Ramada Inn
2701 WNW Loop 323
Tyler, TX 75702
(903) 593-7391

A,H,R,S,NS   **

Marriott Residence Inn
3303 Troup Hwy.
Tyler, TX 75701
(903) 595-5188

A,S,SA   **

SOUTH-CENTRAL

Van Horn
Comfort Inn   G,H,R   *
1601 W. Broadway St.
Van Horn, TX 79855
(915) 283-2211

Rodeway Inn   G,R   *
I-10 & W. US 80
Van Horn, TX 79855
(915) 283-2992

Howard Johnson Lodge   H,R,S,NS   *
200 Golf Course Drive
Van Horn, TX 79855
(915) 283-2780

Vernon
Econo Lodge   G,H,R,T   *
4100 SR 287 N.W.
Vernon, TX 76384
(817) 553-3384

Victoria
Comfort Inn   G,H,R   *
1906 Houston Hwy.
Victoria, TX 77901
(512) 574-9393

Waco
Howard Johnson Lodge   H,R,S,NS   *
101 N. I-35
Waco, TX 76704
(817) 752-8222

Waxahachie
Comfort Inn   H,R   *
200 I-35 E.
Waxahachie, TX 75165
(214) 937-4202

SOUTH-CENTRAL

NORTH-
CENTRAL

NORTH-CENTRAL

Iowa
Minnesota
Nebraska
North Dakota
South Dakota

Hotel Cost Codes (for average one-night stay)

*	$30-60/night
**	$61-100/night
***	$101-150/night
****	$151 and up/night
W	Hotel has weekly rates only

Note: costs may vary by season.

Hotel Amenity Codes

A	Airport nearby
H	Handicapped access
HS	Hair salon on premises
G	Golf within 10 miles
NS	Non-smoking rooms available
OB	Facility is on the beach
P	Playground on premises
R	Restaurant on premises
S	Swimming on premises
SA	Sauna on premises
SK	Skiing within 25 miles
T	Tennis within 10 miles

NORTH-CENTRAL

IOWA

Ames
Comfort Inn   G,H,R,S,T   *
1605 S. Dayton Ave.
Ames, IA 50010
(515) 232-0689

Ramada Inn   A,G,H,R,S,T,NS   *
1206 S Duff
Ames, IA 50010
(515) 232-3410

Atlantic
Econo Lodge   R   *
I-80 & US 71
Atlantic, IA 50022
(712) 243-4067

Burlington
Ramada Inn   A,G,H,R,S,R,NS,SA   *
2759 Mt. Pleasant St.
Burlington, IA 52601
(319) 754-5781

Carroll
Burke Inn   G,H,R,SA   *
1225 Plaza Dr.
Carroll, IA 51401
(712) 792-5156

Cedar Falls
Econo Lodge   G,R,T   *
4117 University Ave.
Cedar Falls, IA 50613
(319) 277-6931

Cedar Rapids
Comfort Inn   G,H,T   *
5055 Rockwell Dr.
Cedar Rapids, IA 52402
(319) 393-8247

Comfort Inn   G,H,R,T   *
390 33rd Ave.
Cedar Rapids, IA 52404
(319) 363-7934

HoJo Inn   R,NS   *
3233 Southridge Drive, SW
Cedar Rapids, IA 52404
(319) 363-9999

Days Inn   N/A   **
3245 Southgate Pl. SW
Cedar Rapids, IA 52404
(319) 365-4339

Clinton
Ramada Inn   G,H,R,S,NS   *
1522 Lincolnway
Clinton, IA 52732
(319) 243-8841

Coralville
Comfort Inn   G,H,R,S,T   **
209 W. 9th St.
Coralville, IA 52241
(319) 351-8144

Econo Lodge   G,H,R   *
815 1st Ave.
Coralville, IA 52241
(319) 354-6000

Des Moines
Budget Host Inn   NS   *
7625 Hickman Rd.
Des Moines, IA 50322

Comfort Inn   G,H,R,S   **
5231 Fleur Dr.
Des Moines, IA 50321
(515) 287-3434

14th Street Inn   A,H,R,S,NS   *
4684 NE 14th Street
Des Moines, IA 50313
(515) 265-5671

Dubuque
Comfort Inn   H,R,S,SK   **
4055 McDonald St.
Dubuque, IA 52002
(319) 556-3006

Ft. Dodge
Comfort Inn   H,R,S,T   *
2938 5th Ave.
Ft. Dodge, IA 50501
(515) 573-3731

Marshalltown
Comfort Inn   G,H,R,S   *
2613 S. Center St.
Marshalltown, IA 50158
(515) 752-6000

North Sioux City
Comfort Inn   G,H,R,S,T   **
115 Streeter Dr.
North Sioux City, IA 57049
(605) 232-3366

Sioux Center
Econo Lodge   G,H   *
86 9th St. Circle
Sioux Center, IA 51250
(712) 722-4000

Urbandale
Comfort Inn   G,H,R,S   *
5900 Sutton Dr.
Urbandale, IA 50322
(515) 270-1037

Econo Lodge   G,H,R,S,T   *
11000 Douglas Ave.
Urbandale, IA 50322
(515) 278-4601

Waterloo
Comfort Inn   G,H,R,S,T   *
1945 LaPorte Rd.
Waterloo, IA 50702
(319) 234-7411

West Liberty
Econo Lodge   R   *
1943 Garfield Ave.
West Liberty, IA 52776
(319) 627-2171

Winterset
The Village View   N/A   **
711 East Hwy 92
Winterset, IA 50273

MINNESOTA

Austin
Rodeway Inn   G,H,R,T,SK   **
3303 Oakland Ave. W.
Austin, MN 55912
(507) 437-7774

NORTH-CENTRAL

Bemidji
Comfort Inn   G,H,R,S,SA,SK   *
3500 Comfort Dr.
Bemidji, MN 56601
(218) 751-7700

Brainerd
Econo Lodge   G,H,R,T,SK   *
2655 US 371 S.
Brainerd, MN 56041
(218) 828-0027

Cass Lake
Trees Resort   S,SA,T   W
RR-2, Box 258
Cass Lake, MN 56633
(218) 335-2471; (800) 35-TREES

View Point Resort   S,G   W
Little Wolf Lake
RR-3, Box 642
Cass Lake, MN 56633
(218) 335-6746

Detroit Lakes
Budget Host Inn   N/A   *
895 Highway 10 E.
Detroit Lakes, MN 56501
(218) 847-4454

Eagan
Marriott Residence Inn N/A   **
3040 Eagandale Place
Eagan, MN 55121
(612) 688-0363

Grand Marais
Econo Lodge   G,H,R,S,SA,SK   **
US 61 E.
Grand Marais, MN 55604
(218) 387-2547

NORTH-CENTRAL

Mankato
Comfort Inn   H,S   **
131 Apache Pl.
Mankato, MN 56001
(507) 388-5107

Marshall
Comfort Inn   G,H,R   **
1511 E. College Dr.
Marshall, MN 56258
(507) 532-3070

Milaca
Rodeway Inn   G,H,R,SK   *
215 10th Ave.
Milaca, MN 56359
(612) 983-2660

Monticello
Comfort Inn   G,H,T   *
200 E. Oakwood Dr.
Monticello, MN 55362
(612) 295-1111

Owatonna
Ramada Inn   G,H,R,S,T,NS,SA   *
1212 I-35
Owatonna, MN 55060
(507) 455-0606

Redwood Falls
Comfort Inn   H,R,T,SA   **
1382 E. Bridge St.
Redwood Falls, MN 56283
(507) 644-5700

Rochester
Quality Inn   G,H,R   **
1620 1st Ave.
Rochester, MN 55904
(507) 282-8091

NORTH-CENTRAL

Econo Lodge   G,R,T   *
519 Third Ave. S.W.
Rochester, MN 55902
(507) 288-1855

Friendship Inn   G,R,S,T,SA,SK   *
166 Fifth St. S.W.
Rochester, MN 55902
(507) 289-1628

Ramada Inn   A,G,H,R,S,NS,SA   *
1625 South Broadway
Rochester, MN 55904
(507) 281-2211

Sauk Centre
Econo Lodge   G,H,R,T,SK   *
I-94 at Sauk Ctr. Exit
Sauk Centre, MN 56378
(612) 352-6581

Savage
Comfort Inn   H,R,S,SK   **
4601 W. SR 13
Savage, MN 53378
(612) 894-6124

NEBRASKA

Auburn
Auburn Inn Motel   N/A   **
US 75 North, 517 J Street
Auburn, NE 68305
(402) 274-3143

Palmer House Motel   N/A   **
Hwys 73/75 South
1918 J Street
Auburn, NE 68305
(402) 274-3193

NORTH-CENTRAL

Burwell

Calamus River Lodge	R	**
Calamus Lake Rd.		
HC 79 Box 18A		
Burwell, NE 68823		
(308) 346-4331		

Rodeo Inn	S	**
Hwys 91 & 11, P.O. Box 475		
Burwell, NE 68823-0475		
(308) 346-4408		

Council Bluffs

Econo Lodge	G,H,R,SK	*
3208 S. 7th St.		
Council Bluffs, NE 51501		
(712) 366-9699		

Cozad

Budget Host Circle S Motel	NS,R,S	*
440 S. Meridian, P.O. Box 85		
Cozad, NE 69130		
(308) 784-2290		

Fremont

Comfort Inn	G,H,R,S	*
1649 E. 23rd St.		
Fremont, NE 68025		
(402) 721-1109		

Grand Island

Oak Grove Inn	NS	**
3205 S. Locust Street		
Grand Island, NE 68801		
(308) 384-1333; (800) 435-7144		

Conoco Motel	NS,S,R	**
2107 West Second St.		
Grand Island, NE 68802		
(308) 384-2700		

Lazy V Motel   S   **
2703 East Hwy 30
Grand Island, NE 68801
(308) 384-0700

Lexington
Econo Lodge   R,S,T   *
I-80 at US 283
Lexington, NE 68850
(308) 324-5601

Lincoln
Comfort Suites   H,S   *
4231 Industrial Ave.
Lincoln, NE 68504
(402) 476-8080

Comfort Inn   H,R,SA   *
2940 N.W. 12th St.
Lincoln, NE 68521
(402) 475-2200

Econo Lodge   G,R   *
5600 Cornhusker Hwy.
Lincoln, NE 68529
(402) 464-5971

Marriott Residence Inn   N/A   **
200 S. 68th Place
Lincoln, NE 68510
(402) 483-4900

Ramada Inn Airport   A,G,H,R,S,NS   *
2301 NW 12th Street
Lincoln, NE 68521
(402) 475-4400

Neligh
DeLuxe Motel   N/A   **
Hwy 275 E., P.O. Box 113
Neligh, NE 68756
(402) 887-4628

NORTH-CENTRAL

West Hillview Motel   NS   **
West Hwy 275, Rt. 2 Box 43
Neligh, NE 68756
(402) 887-4186

Norfolk
Ramada Inn   A,G,H,R,S,NS   *
1227 Omaha Ave.
Norfolk, NE 68701
(402) 371-7000

Omaha
Clarion Hotel   G,H,R,S   **
10909 M St.
Omaha, NE 68137
(402) 331-8220

Comfort Inn   G,H,R,S   *
10919 J St.
Omaha, NE 68137
(402) 592-2882

Marriott Residence Inn   A,S,SA   **
6990 Dodge St.
Omaha, NE 68132
(402) 553-8898

Ramada Hotel Central I-80   A,H,R,S,NS,SA   *
7007 Grover Street
Omaha, NE 68106
(402) 397-7030

Ramada Inn Airport   A,G,H,S,NS,SA   *
Abbott Dr & Locust St
Omaha, NE 68110
(402) 342-5100

O'Neill
Budget Host Carriage House   N/A   *
929 E. Douglas, Box 151
O'Neill, NE 68763
(402) 336-3403

NORTH-CENTRAL

Sioux City
Econo Lodge   G,H,R,T   *
4402 Dakota Ave.
South Sioux City, NE 68776
(402) 494-4114

NORTH DAKOTA

Bismarck
Bismarck Hotel   A,H,R,S,HS,NS,SA   *
1215 West Main
Bismarck, ND 58504
(701) 223-9600

Bowman
Budget Host 4-U Motel   G,R,SA   *
704 Highway 12 W, Box 590
Bowman, ND 58623
(701) 523-3243

Cavalier
Cedar Inn   R   **
Hwy 18 S.
Cavalier, ND
(701) 265-8341

Devils Lake
Comfort Inn   G,H,R,S   *
215 US 2 E.
Devils Lake, ND 58301
(701) 662-6760

Dickinson
Comfort Inn   G,H,R,S   *
493 Elk Dr.
Dickinson, ND 58601
(701) 264-7300

NORTH-CENTRAL

Rodeway Inn   G,R,T   *
1000 W. Villard
Dickinson, ND 58601
(701) 225-6703

Fargo
Comfort Inn   G,H,R,S,T   *
3825 9th Ave., S.W.
Fargo, ND 58103
(701) 282-9596

Comfort Suites   G,H,R,S   **
1415 35th St.
Fargo, ND 58103
(701) 237-5911

Comfort Inn   G,H,R,S   *
1407 35th St.
Fargo, ND 58103
(701) 280-9666

Econo Lodge   G,H,R,T   *
1401 35th St.
Fargo, ND 58103
(701) 232-3412

Grand Forks
Comfort Inn   G,H,R,S,T   *
3251 30th Ave.
Grand Forks, ND 58201
(701) 775-7503

Comfort Inn   H,R,S   *
US 2 East
East Grand Forks, ND 56721
(218) 773-9545

Econo Lodge   G,H,R,T   *
900 N. 43rd St.
Grand Forks, ND 58201
(701) 746-6666

NORTH-CENTRAL

Garrison

Garrison Motel   N/A   **
Hwy 37
Garrison, ND
(701) 463-2858

Jamestown

Comfort Inn   H,R,S   *
811 20th St., S.W.
Jamestown, ND 58401
(701) 252-7125

Minot

Comfort Inn   G,H,R,S   *
1515 22nd Ave.
Minot, ND 58701
(701) 852-2201

Rugby

Econo Lodge   G,R,S   *
US 2 East
Rugby, ND 58368
(701) 776-5776

Wahpeton

Comfort Inn   G,H,R,S,T   *
209 13th St.
Wahpeton, ND 58075
(701) 642-1115

Icelandic State Park
Camping Information
(701) 265-4561

SOUTH DAKOTA

Badlands National Park/Interior
Badlands Budget Host Motel   S   *
HC54, Box 115
Interior, SD 57750
(605) 433-5335
NOTE: Closed fall/winter

Keystone
Brookside Motel   N/A   **
603 Reed St.
P.O. Box 137
Keystone, SD 57751
(800) 551-9381
(605) 666-4496

Rapid City
Comfort Inn   G,H,R,S,T   **
1550 N. LaCrosse
Rapid City, SD 57701
(605) 348-2221

Econo Lodge   G,H,R,S,T   **
625 E. Disk Dr.
Rapid City, SD 57701
(605) 342-6400

Howard Johnson Lodge   H,R,S,NS   *
Box 1795
2211 LaCrosse Street
Rapid City, SD 57709
(605) 343-8550

Ramada Inn   G,H,R,S,T,NS   *
1721 Lacrosse St.
Rapid City, SD 57701
(605) 342-1300

Quality Inn   G,H,R,T,SK   **
2208 Mt. Rushmore Rd.
Rapid City, SD 57709
(605) 342-3322

Sioux Falls
Comfort Suites   G,H,R,S,T,SK   **
3208 S. Carolyn Ave.
Sioux Falls, SD 57106
(605) 362-9711

Vermillion
Budget Host Tomahawk Motel   S   *
1313 W. Cherry St.
Vermillion, SD 57069
(605) 624-2601

Comfort Inn   G,R,T   *
701 W. Cherry St.
Vermillion, SD 57069
(605) 624-8333

Watertown
Comfort Inn   H,R,S   **
800 35th St.
Watertown, SD 57201
(605) 886-3010

Budget Host Inn   NS,R   *
309 8th Avenue SE
Watertown, SD 57201
(605) 886-8455

Yankton
Comfort Inn   G,H,R,T   *
2118 Broadway
Yankton, SD 57078
(605) 665-8053

NORTH-CENTRAL

Pet-friendly Campgrounds
Happy Holiday Campground/Rapid City
Lazy 'J' Campground/Rapid City
Grace Coolidge, Custer State Park/Custer

SOUTHWEST

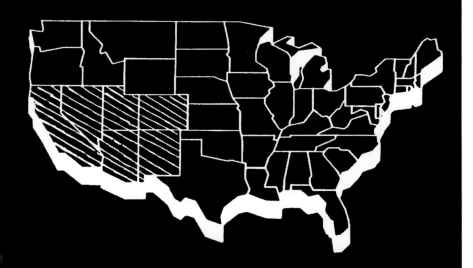

SOUTHWEST

Arizona
California
Colorado
Nevada
New Mexico
Utah

Hotel Cost Codes (for average one-night stay)

*	$30-60/night
**	$61-100/night
***	$101-150/night
****	$151 and up/night
W	Hotel has weekly rates only

Note: costs may vary by season.

Hotel Amenity Codes

A	Airport nearby
H	Handicapped access
HS	Hair salon on premises
G	Golf within 10 miles
NS	Non-smoking rooms available
OB	Facility is on the beach
P	Playground on premises
R	Restaurant on premises
S	Swimming on premises
SA	Sauna on premises
SK	Skiing within 25 miles
T	Tennis within 10 miles

ARIZONA

Flagstaff
Marriott Residence Inn 3440 N. Country Club Drive Flagstaff, AZ 86004 (520) 526-5555	G,R,SK	***

Quality Inn 2000 S. Milton Rd. Flagstaff, AZ 86001 (602) 774-8771	G,R,T,SK	**

Comfort Inn 914 S. Milton Rd. Flagstaff, AZ 86001 (602) 774-7326	G,H,R,SK	*

Holbrook
Econo Lodge 2596 Navajo Blvd. Holbrook, AZ 86025 (602) 524-1448	G,H,R	*

Howard Johnson Navajo Blvd. Holbrook, AZ 86025 OPENING SOON	H,R,S,NS	*

Comfort Inn 2602 E. Navajo Blvd. Holbrook, AZ 86025 (602) 524-6131	G,H,R,T	*

Ramada Limited 2608 E. Navajo Blvd. Holbrook, AZ 86025 (520) 524-2566	S,H,G,R,NS	**

Green Valley
Quality Inn   G,H,R   **
11 S. La Canada
Green Valley, AZ 85614
(520) 625-2250

Page
Econo Lodge   G,R,T   *
121 S. Lake Powell Blvd.
Page, AZ 86040
(520) 645-2488

Phoenix
Marriott Residence Inn   N/A   ***
8242 N. Black Canyon Freeway
Phoenix, AZ 85051
(602) 864-1900

Rodeway Inn   G,H,R   *
1550 S. 52nd St.
Phoenix, AZ 85281
(602) 967-3000

Econo Lodge   H,R   **
1520 N. 84th Dr.
Phoenix, AZ 85353
(602) 936-4667

Howard Johnson Lodge   A,R,S,NS   *
124 So. 24th St.
Phoenix, AZ 85034
(602) 244-8221

Quality Inn   G,H,R   **
5121 E. La Puente Ave.
Phoenix, AZ 85044
(602) 893-3900

Quality Hotel   G,H,R,T   **
3600 N. 2nd Ave.
Phoenix, AZ 85013
(602) 248-0222

SOUTHWEST

Econo Lodge 3541 E. Van Buren Pkwy. Phoenix, AZ 85008 (602) 273-7121	G,R,T	*
Holiday Inn 5300 S. Priest St. Phoenix, AZ 85283 (602) 820-7500	G,R,T	*
Howard Johnson 3400 Grand Ave. Phoenix, AZ 85017 (602) 264-9164	G,H,R,T	*

Pinetop

Econo Lodge 458 White Mountain Blvd. Pinetop, AZ 85935 (520) 367-3636	G,H,R,T,SK	*

Scottsdale

Marriott Residence Inn 6040 N. Scottsdale Rd. Scottsdale, AZ 85253 (602) 948-8666	G, R, SA	***
Inn at the Citadel 8700 E. Pinnacle Peak Rd. Scottsdale, AZ 85255 (602) 585-6133; (800) 927-8367	N/A	****

Sedona

Quality Inn 771 SR 179 Sedona, AZ 86339 (520) 282-7151	G,H,R,T	**

Tempe
Marriott Residence Inn   G,R, SA   ***
5075 S. Priest Drive
Tempe, AZ 85282
(602) 756-2122

Tucson
Marriott Residence Inn   G   ***
647 E. Speedway Blvd.
Tucson, AZ 85710
(520) 721-0991

Ramada Inn Foothills 3   S,H,G,T,SA,NS   **
6944 E. Tanque Verde
Tucson, AZ 85715
(602) 886-9595

Clarion Hotel   H,R   **
6801 S. Tucson Blvd.
Tucson, AZ 85706
(520) 746-3932

Rodeway Inn   G,H,R,SK   **
1365 W. Grant Rd.
Tucson, AZ 85745
(602) 622-7791

Rodeway Inn   G,R,T   *
810 E. Benson Hwy.
Tucson, AZ 85713
(602) 884-5800

Red Roof Inn   N/A   **
3700 E. Irvington Rd.
Tucson, AZ 85714
(602) 571-1400

Radisson Suite Tuscon   N/A   ***
6555 E. Speedway Blvd.
Tuscon, AZ 85710
(602) 721-7100

SOUTHWEST

Willcox
Days Inn   G,H,R   **
724 N. Bisbee Ave.
Willcox, AZ 85643
(520) 384-4222

Williams
Ramada Inn (at the M.S.)   S,A,H,G,T,R,NS   ***
642 E. Bill Williams Ave.
Williams, AZ 86046
(520) 635-4431

Winslow
Comfort Inn   G,H,R,S   *
520 Desmond St.
Winslow, AZ 86047
(602) 289-9581

CALIFORNIA

Anaheim
Quality Hotel   G,H,R,T   **
616 Convention Way
Anaheim, CA 92802
(714) 750-3131

Arcata
Quality Inn   G,H,R,T   *
3535 Janes Rd.
Arcata, CA 95521
(707) 822-0409

Arcadia
Hampton Inn   G   **
311 E. Huntington Dr.
Arcadia, CA 91006
(818) 574-5600

Bakersfield
Marriott Residence Inn   R   **
4241 Chester Lane
Bakersfield, CA 93309
(805) 321-9800

Econo Lodge   G,H,R   *
200 Trask St.
Bakersfield, CA 93312
(805) 764-5221

Barstow
Econo Lodge   G,R   *
1230 E. Main St.
Barstow, CA 92311
(619) 256-2113

Comfort Inn   H,R,S,NS   **
1431 East Main Street
Barstow, CA 92311
(619) 256-0661

Beaumont
Budget Host Golden West Motel   R,S   *
625 E. 5th St.
Beaumont, CA 92223
(909) 845-2185

Bishop
Rodeway Inn   G,R,T   *
150 E. Elm St.
Bishop, CA 93514
(619) 873-3564

Buellton
Econo Lodge   G,H,R,T   *
630 Ave. of Flags
Buellton, CA 93427
(805) 688-0022

Carmel
The Cypress Inn   N/A   ***
7th Ave. & Lincoln
Carmel, CA 93921
(800) 443-7443

Castaic
Comfort Inn   G,H,R   *
31558 Castaic Rd.
Castaic, CA 91384
(805) 295-1100

Chico
Woodcrest Inn   H,R,SA   *
400 C St., P.O. Box 729
Williams, CA 95987
(916) 473-2381

Vagabond Inn   G,R   *
630 Main St.
Chico, CA 95928
(916) 895-1323

Claremont
Howard Johnson Lodge   A,H,R,S,NS   *
721 South Indian Hill Blvd
Claremont, CA 91711
(909) 626-2431

Costa Mesa
Marriott Residence Inn   R   **
881 Baker Street
Costa Mesa, CA 92626
(714) 241-8800

Ramada Limited   S,A,H,G,T,NS   **
(Newport Beach Area)
1680 Superior Ave.
Costa Mesa, CA 92627
(714) 645-2221

SOUTHWEST

Danville
Danville Inn   G,H,R   **
803 Camino Ramon
Danville, CA 94526
(510) 838-8080

Davis
Econo Lodge   G,H,R,T   *
221 D St.
Davis, CA 95616
(916) 756-1040

Delano
Comfort Inn   G,H,R   *
2211 Girard St.
Delano, CA 93215
(805) 725-1022

Eureka
Vagabond Inn   G,R   *
1630 Fourth St.
Eureka, CA 95501
(707) 443-8041

Fountain Valley
Marriott Residence Inn   R   ***
9930 Slater Ave.
Fountain Valley, CA 92708
(714) 965-8000

Fremont
Marriott Residence Inn   R   **
5400 Farwell Place
Fremont, CA 94536
(510) 794-5900

Fresno
Marriott Residence Inn   R   **
5322 N. Diana Ave.
Fresno, CA 93710
(209) 222-8900

SOUTHWEST

Half Moon Bay
Ramada Limited   A,H,G,T,NS   ***
3020 Cabrillo Hwy (1)
Half Moon Bay, CA 94019
(415)726-9700

Hemet
Ramada Inn   S,G,R,SA,NS   *
3885 W. Florida Ave.
Hemet, CA 92545
(909) 929-8900

Indio
Comfort Inn   G,T   *
43505 Monroe St.
Indio, CA 92201
(619) 347-4044

Inglewood
Econo Lodge   G,H,R   *
439 W. Manchester Blvd.
Inglewood, CA 90301
(310) 674-8596

Econo Lodge   G,H,R   *
4123 W. Century Blvd.
Inglewood, CA 90304
(310) 672-7285

Irvine
Marriott Residence Inn   R   ***
10 Morgan St.
Irvine, CA 92618
(714) 380-3000

La Mesa
Comfort Inn   G,H,R   **
8000 Parkway Dr.
La Mesa, CA 91942
(619) 698-7747

SOUTHWEST

La Mirada-Buena Park
Marriott Residence Inn   R   ***
14419 Firestone Blvd.
La Mirada, CA 90638
(714) 523-2800

Livermore
Marriott Residence Inn   G, R, SA,S   ***
1000 Airway Blvd.
Livermore, CA 94550
(510) 373-1800

Lodi
Comfort Inn   G,H,R   **
118 N. Cherokee Ln.
Lodi, CA 95240
(209) 367-4848

Lompoc
Quality Inn   G,H,R,T   **
1621 N. H St.
Lompoc, CA 93436
(805) 735-8555

Long Beach
Marriott Residence Inn   R,S,G,SA   ***
4111 E. Willow St.
Long Beach, CA 90815
(310) 595-0909

Guest House Hotel   S,A,G,T,NS   ***
5325 E. Pac.Coast Hwy.
Long Beach, CA 90804
(310) 597-1341

Los Angeles
Marriott Residence Inn   R, S, SA   ***
1700 N. Sepulveda Blvd.
Manhattan Beach, CA 90266
(310) 546-7627

SOUTHWEST

Comfort Inn   G,R,T   *
2804 E. Garvey Ave.
Los Angeles, CA 91791
(818) 915-6077

Mojave
Vagabond Inn   G,R   *
2145 SR 58
Mojave, CA 93501
(805) 824-2463

Mountain View
Marriott Residence Inn   R, S   ***
1854 El Camino Real West
Mountain View, CA 94040
(415) 940-1300

Oakland
Clarion Suites Hotel   G,H,R,T   **
1800 Madison St.
Oakland, CA 94612
(510) 832-2300

Ontario
Marriott Residence Inn   R, S   ***
2025 Convention Center Way
Ontario, CA 91764
(909) 983-6788

Oroville
Econo Lodge   G,R,T   **
1835 Feather River Blvd.
Oroville, CA 95965
(916) 533-8201

Oxnard
Friendship Inn   G,R,T   *
1021 S. Oxnard Blvd.
Oxnard, CA 93030
(805) 486-8381

SOUTHWEST

Pasadena
Comfort Inn   G,R   **
2462 E. Colorado
Pasadena, CA 91107
(818) 405-0811

Petaluma
Quality Inn   G,H,R   **
5100 Montero Way
Petaluma, CA 94954
(707) 664-1155

Pismo Beach
Oxford Suites   G,H,R,T   **
651 Five Cities Dr.
Pismo Beach, CA 93449
(805) 773-3773

Placentia
Marriott Residence Inn   N/A   ***
700 W. Kimberly Ave
Placentia, CA 92870
(714) 996-0555

Pleasant Hill
Marriott Residence Inn   N/A   ***
700 Ellinwood Way
Pleasant Hill, CA 94523
(510) 689-1010

Rancho Cordova
Comfort Inn   G,H,R,T   **
3240 Mather Field Rd.
Rancho Cordova, CA 95670
(916) 363-3344

Redding
Comfort Inn   G,H,R,T   *
2059 Hilltop Dr.
Redding, CA 96002
(916) 221-6530

SOUTHWEST

Vagabond Inn   G,R,T   *
2010 Pine St.
Redding, CA 96001
(916) 243-3336

Reseda
Howard Johnson Lodge   H,R,S,NS   *
7432 Reseda Blvd.
Reseda, CA 91335
(818) 344-0324

Riverside
Econo Lodge   G,R,T   *
1971 University Ave.
Riverside, CA 92507
(909) 684-6363

Sacramento
Clarion Hotel   G,H,R,T   **
700 16th St.
Sacramento, CA 95814
(916) 444-8000

Vagabond Inn   R,T   *
1319 30th St.
Sacramento, CA 95816
(916) 454-4400

Marriott Residence Inn   A,S,SA   ***
2410 W. El Camino Ave.
Sacramento, CA 95833
(916) 649-1300

Howard Johnson Hotel   H,R,NS   **
3343 Bradshaw Road
Sacramento, CA 95827
(916) 366-1266

SOUTHWEST

San Diego

Econo Lodge   G,R,OB   **
445 S. Hotel Circle
San Diego, CA 92108
(619) 692-1288

Hilton Beach & Tennis Resort   R,T   ***
1775 E. Mission Bay Drive
San Diego, CA 92109
(619) 276-4010

Red Lion Inn   N/A   ***
7450 Hazard Center Drive
San Diego, CA 92108
(619) 297-5466

U.S. Grant Hotel   N/A   ***
326 Broadway
San Diego, CA 92101
(619) 232-3121

*** San Diego Visitors can get info from Dog Beach Dog Wash
*** http://www.dogwash.com
***(619) 523-1700

San Francisco

Vagabond Inn   H,R   **
222 S. Airport Blvd.
San Francisco, CA 94080
(415) 589-9055

Econo Lodge   G,R,T   **
2930 El Camino Real
San Jose, CA 95051
(408) 241-3010

Ramada Inn SF AP (N6)   S,A,R,NS   **
245 S. Airport Blvd.
San Francisco, CA 94080
(415) 589-7200

SOUTHWEST

Travelodge   G,H,R,T   **
1450 Lombard St.
San Francisco, CA 94123
(415) 673-0691

Hilton & Towers   R   ***
333 O'Farrell Sty.
San Francisco, CA 94102
(415) 771-1400

Marriott Fisherman's Wharf   R   ***
1250 Columbus Ave.
San Francisco, CA 94102
(415) 775-7555

Beresford Arms   R   **
635 Sutter St.
San Francisco, CA 94102
(800) 533-6533

Mansions Hotel   R   ***
2220 Sacramento St.
San Francisco, CA 94102
(415) 929-9444

Four Seasons Clift   R   ****
495 Geary St.
San Francisco, CA 94102
(415) 775-4700

Haus Kleebauer B&B   R   **
San Francisco
(415) 621-0482

San Mateo
Villa Hotel   G,H,R   **
4000 S. El Camino Real
San Mateo, CA 94403
(415) 341-0966

SOUTHWEST

Marriott Residence Inn   A,S,SA   ***
2000 Winward Way
San Mateo, CA 94404
(415) 574-4700

Santa Maria
Comfort Inn   A,H,S,NS   *
210 South Nicholson Avenue
Santa Maria, CA 93454
(805) 922-5891

Sunnyvale
Marriott Residence Inn   N/A   ***
750 Lakeway
Sunnyvale, CA 94086
(408) 720-1000

Temecula
Ramada Inn Wine Ctry So.   S,H,G,T,NS   *
28980 Front Street
Temecula, CA 92590
(909) 676-8770

Torrance
Marriott Residence Inn   A,S,SA   ***
3701 Torrance Blvd.
Torrance, CA 90503
(310) 543-4566

Tulare
Friendship Inn   G,R,T   *
26442 SR 99
Tulare, CA 93274
(209) 688-0501

COLORADO

Aspen

Hotel Jerome 330 East Main St. Aspen, CO 81611 (970) 920-1000	S,R,T	***
Cresthaus Lodge 1301 East Cooper Aspen, CO 81611 (970) 925-7081	S,SA	***
Limelite Lodge 228 East Cooper Aspen, CO 81611 (970) 925-3025	N/A	***

Avon

Comfort Inn 0161 W. Beaver Creek Blvd. Avon, CO 81620 (303) 949-5511	G,H,R,T,SK	**

Boulder

Marriott Residence Inn 3030 Center Green Dr. Boulder, CO 80301 (303) 449-5545	N/A	**

Brush

Budget Host Empire Motel 1408 Edison Brush, CO 80723 (970) 842-2876	NS,R	*

Colorado Springs

Ramada Inn North 4440 N I-25 Colorado Springs, CO 80907 (719) 594-0700	G,H,R,S,NS,SK	*

SOUTHWEST

Marriott Residence Inn   N/A   **
2765 Geyser Drive
Colorado Springs, CO 80906
(719) 576-0101

Rodeway Inn   G,R,T   *
2409 E. Pikes Peak
Colorado Springs, CO 80909
(719) 471-0990

Cortez
Comfort Inn   G,H,S,T   *
2308 E. Main
P.O. Box 1048
Cortez, CO 81321
(303) 565-3400

Denver
Comfort Inn   G,H,R   *
7201 E. 36th Ave.
Denver, CO 80207
(303) 393-7666

Ramada Inn 7   G,R,S,T,NS   *
1975 Bryant Street
Denver, CO 80204
(303) 433-8331

Ramada Inn Airport 1   A,G,H,R,S,NS   *
3737 Quebec Street
Denver, CO 80207
(303) 388-6161

Ramada Inn Downtown 3   A,G,H,R,S,T,NS   *
1150 E. Colfax
Denver, CO 80216
(303) 831-7700

Rodeway Inn   G,H,R,SK   *
7150 W. Colfax Ave.
Denver, CO 80215
(303) 238-1251

Marriott Residence Inn   A,S,SA   ***
2777 Zuni St.
Denver, CO 80211
(303) 458-5318

Quality Inn   G,H,R,SA   **
6300 E. Hampden Ave.
Denver, CO 80222
(303) 758-2211

Durango
Rodeway Inn   G,R,S,T,SK   **
2701 Main Ave.
Durango, CO 81301
(303) 259-2540

Ft. Collins
Plaza Inn   A,G,H,R,S,T,NS,SA   *
3709 E Mulberry Street
Ft. Collins, CO 80524
(970) 493-7800

Sleep Inn   H,R   *
3808 Mulberry St.
Ft. Collins, CO 80524
(303) 484-0814

Ft. Morgan
Econo Lodge   G,R,T   **
1409 Barlow Rd.
Ft. Morgan, CO 80701
(303) 867-9481

Glenwood Springs
Ramada Inn   G,H,R,S,T,NS,SK   *
124 West 6th Street
Glenwood Springs, CO 81601
(970) 945-2500

SOUTHWEST

Grand Junction
Howard Johnson Lodge   A,H,R,S,NS   *
752 Horizon Drive
Grand Junction, CO 81506
(970) 243-5150

La Junta
Quality Inn   G,R,T   *
1325 E. 3rd St., P.O. Box 1180
La Junta, CO 81050
(719) 384-2571

Lakewood
Comfort Inn   G,H,R   **
3440 S. Vance St.
Lakewood, CO 80277
(303) 989-5500

Best Western   G,H,R,S,T,NS,SK   *
11595 West 6th Avenue
Lakewood, CO 80215
(303) 238-7751

Leadville
Silver King   SK,R   **
2020 N. Popular
Leadville, CO 80461
(800) 871-2610

Timberline/ Mt. Peaks   SK   **
216 Harrison Ave.
Leadville, CO
(800) 352-1876

The Bel Air   N/A   **
231 Elm St.
Leadville, CO 80461
(719) 486-0881

SOUTHWEST

The Alps   N/A   **
207 Elm St.
Leadville, CO 80461
(800) 818-2577

Limon
Econo Lodge   G,R   *
I-70 & US 24, P.O. Box 925
Limon, CO 80828
(719) 775-2867

Monte Vista
Comfort Inn   G,H,R,S,T,SA   *
1519 Grande Ave.
Monte Vista, CO 81144
(719) 852-0612

Sterling
Ramada Inn   G,H,R,S,T,NS,SA   *
I-76 & US Hwy 6
Sterling, CO 80751
(970) 522-2625

Telluride
The Peaks   R,S,T,G   ****
136 Country Club Drive
P.O.Box 2702
Telluride, CO 81435
(800) 789-2220

Wheat Ridge
Quality Inn   G,H,R,T   *
12100 W. 44th Ave.
Wheat Ridge, CO 80033
(303) 467-2400

SOUTHWEST

NEVADA

Las Vegas
King Albert Inn   R,T   **
185 Albert Ave.
Las Vegas, NV 89109
(702) 735-1741

Marriott Residence Inn   A,R,S,SA   ***
3225 Paradise Rd.
Las Vegas, NV 89109
(702) 796-9300

Reno
Marriott Residence Inn   A,S   ***
9845 Gateway Dr.
Reno, NV 89511
(702) 853-8800

Travelodge   G,H,R,T,SA   **
2050 Market St.
Reno, NV 89502
(702) 786-2500

Campgrounds/RV Parks (All of these have both)

The following is just a sampling. Many of these hundreds of parks
allow pets. Check with the Nevada Tourism Board for other areas if
you need them.

Pioneer Territory
R Place
Hwy 93, HCR 61, Box 28B
Hiko, NV 89017
(702) 725-3545

Bailey's Hot Springs
Hwy 95
Beatty, NV 89003
(702) 553-2395

SOUTHWEST

Burro Inn
Hwy 95
Beatty, NV 89003
(702) 553-2225; (800) 843-2078

Space Station RV Park
Hwy 95
Beatty, NV 89003
(702) 533-9039

Agua Caliente
Hwy 93
Caliente, NV 89008
(702) 725-3114

Young's RV Park
Hwy 93
Caliente, NV 89008
(702) 726-3418

Reno-Tahoe Territory
Camp'N Town
2438 N. Carson St.
Carson City, NV 89706
(702) 883-1123; (800) 872-1123

Comstock Country RV Resort
5400 N. Carson St.
Carson City, NV 89701
(702) 882-2445

Pony Express Territory
Austin RV Park
Hwy 50
Austin, NV 89310
(702) 964-2393

The Y
Hwy 50 & SR 487
Baker, NV 89311
(702) 234-7223

SOUTHWEST

Whispering Elms RV Park
State Hwy 487
Baker, NV 89311
(702) 234-7343

Cowboy Country
Denio Junction
P.O. Box 7035
Denio, NV 89404
(702) 941-0371

Royal Peacock Opal
P.O. Box 55, Virgin Valley
Denio, NV 89404
(702) 941-0374

Rydon Campground
I-80, P.O. Box 1656
Elko, NV 90801
(702) 738-3448

Hidden Valley Guest & RV Resort
I-80, P.O. Box 1454
Elko, NV 90801
(702) 738-2347

NEW MEXICO

Albuquerque

Comfort Inn	G,R,SK		*
13031 Central Ave.			
Albuquerque, NM 87123			
(505) 294-1800			

Comfort Inn	G,H,R		*
2300 Yale Blvd.			
Albuquerque, NM 87106			
(505) 243-2244			

King Allen Inn   R-1

Econo Lodge   H,R,T,SA,SK   *
13211 Central Ave. NE
Albuquerque, NM 87123
(505) 292-7600

HoJo Inn   A,H,R,NS   *
7640 Central S.E.
Albuquerque, NM 87108
(505) 265-9309

Marriott Residence Inn   A,S,SA   ***
3300 Prospect Ave. NE
Albuquerque, NM 87107
(505) 881-2661

Ramada Inn East   A,G,H,R,S,T,NS,SK   **
25 Hotel Circle NE
Albuquerque, NM 87123
(505) 271-1000

Rodeway Inn   G,R,SK   *
12901 Central NE
Albuquerque, NM 87108
(800) 228-2000

Carlsbad
Great Western Inn   R,S,T,SA   *
3804 National Parks Hwy.
Carlsbad, NM 88220
(505) 887-5535

Quality Inn   G,H,R   **
3706 National Parks Hwy.
Carlsbad, NM 88220
(505) 887-2861

Espanola
Comfort Inn   H,R,S,SK   *
247 S. Riverside Dr.
Espanola, NM 87532
(505) 753-2419

SOUTHWEST

Gallup
Comfort Inn   G,H,R,S   *
3208 W. US 66
Gallup, NM 87301
(505) 722-0982

Econo Lodge   R   *
3101 W. US 66
Gallup, NM 87301
(505) 722-3800

Sleep Inn   G,H,R,S   *
3820 E. Historic US 66
Gallup, NM 87301
(800) 221-2222

Las Cruces
Comfort Inn   G,R   *
2485 S. Valley Dr.
Las Cruces, NM 88005
(800) 228-5150

Roswell
Comfort Inn   G,H,R   *
3581 Main St.
Roswell, NM 88201
(800) 228-5150

Santa Fe
Marriott Residence Inn   A,G,S,SA   ***
1698 Galisteo St.
Santa Fe, NM 87505
(505) 988-7300

Ramada Inn   G,H,R,S,NS,SK   **
2907 Cerillos Road
Sante Fe, NM 87501
(505) 471-3000

Quality Inn 3011 Cerrillos Rd. Santa Fe, NM 87501 (505) 471-1211	G,H,R,SK	**

Tucumcari

Comfort Inn 2800 E. Tucumcari Blvd. Tucumcari, NM 88401 (505) 461-4094	G,H,R,T	*
Budget Host Motel 1620 E. Tucumcari Blvd. Tucumcari, NM 88401 (505) 461-1212	G,NS,R	*
Econo Lodge 3400 E. Tucumcari Blvd. Tucumcari, NM 88401 (505) 461-4194	G,H,R	*
Friendship Inn 315 E. Tucumcari Blvd. Tucumcari, NM 88401 (505) 461-0330	G,H,R,T	*
Rodeway Inn 1302 W. Tucumcari Blvd. Tucumcari, NM 88401 (505) 461-3140	G,R	*
Rodeway Inn 1023 E. Tucumcari Blvd. Tucumcari, NM 88401 (505) 461-0360	G,R,T	*

UTAH

Brigham City
HoJo Inn   H,R,S,NS   *
1167 S. Main
Brigham City, UT 84302
(801) 723-8511

Cedar City
Comfort Inn   G,H,R,T,SK   *
250 N., 1100 W.
Cedar City, UT 84720
(801) 586-2082

Rodeway Inn   G,R,T,SK   *
281 S. Main
Cedar City, UT 84720
(801) 586-9916

Green River
Budget Host Lodge   A,G,NS,R,S   **
395 E. Main, Box 545
Green River, UT 84525
(801) 564-3406

Moab
Comfort Suites   G,H,R,S   **
800 S. Main St.
Moab, UT 84532
(801) 259-5252

Ramada Inn   G,H,R,S,T,NS,SA   *
182 S Main St
Moab, UT 84532
(801) 259-7141

Price
Budget Host Inn   NS,S   *
145 N. Carbonville Rd.
Price, UT 84501
(801) 637-2424

SOUTHWEST

Provo

Comfort Inn 1555 Canyon Rd. Provo, UT 84604 (801) 374-6020	G,H,R,S,SK	**
Marriott Residence Inn 252 West 2230 North Provo, UT 84604 (801) 374-1000	A,S	**

Salina

Henry's Hideaway 60 North State Salina, UT 84654 (801) 529-7467	R,S,NS	*

Salt Lake City

Econo Lodge 715 W. North Temple Salt Lake City, UT 84116 (801) 363-0062	G,H,R,T,SK	*
Ramada Inn Downtown 230 West 600 South Salt Lake City, UT 84101 (801) 364-5200	A,H,R,S,NS,SK	**
Quality Inn 4465 Century Dr. Salt Lake City, UT 84123 (801) 268-2533	G,R,SK	**
Marriott Residence Inn 765 E. 400 South Salt Lake City, UT 84102 (801) 532-5511	A,G,S,SA	***

SOUTHWEST

Sandy
Marriott Residence Inn   A,S   ***
270 W. 10000 South
Sandy, UT 84070
(801) 561-5005

St. George
Econo Lodge   G,R,T,SA   *
460 E. St. George Blvd.
St. George, UT 84770
(801) 673-4861

Travelodge East   R   **
175 N. 1000 East St.
St. George, UT 84770
(801) 673-4621

NORTHWEST

NORTHWEST

Idaho
Montana
Oregon
Washington
Wyoming

Hotel Cost Codes (for average one-night stay)

*	$30-60/night
**	$61-100/night
***	$101-150/night
****	$151 and up/night
W	Hotel has weekly rates only

Note: costs may vary by season.

Hotel Amenity Codes

A	Airport nearby
H	Handicapped access
HS	Hair salon on premises
G	Golf within 10 miles
NS	Non-smoking rooms available
OB	Facility is on the beach
P	Playground on premises
R	Restaurant on premises
S	Swimming on premises
SA	Sauna on premises
SK	Skiing within 25 miles
T	Tennis within 10 miles

IDAHO

Boise
Quality Inn 2717 Vista Ave. Boise, ID 83705 (208) 343-7505	G,H,R,SK	**
Marriott Residence Inn 1401 Lusk Boise, ID 83706 (208) 344-1200	N/A	***

Caldwell
Comfort Inn 901 Specht Ave. Caldwell, ID 83605 (208) 454-2222	R,S,SA	**

Coeur D'Alene
Comfort Inn 280 W. Appleway Coeur D'Alene, ID 83814 (208) 765-5500	H,R,SA	*

Idaho Falls
Comfort Inn I-95 S. Colorado Ave. Idaho Falls, ID 83402 (208) 528-2804	R	**
Quality Inn 850 Lindsay Blvd. Idaho Falls, ID 83402 (208) 523-6260	G,R	*

Ketchum
Clarion Inn 600 Main St. Ketchum, ID 83340 (208) 726-5900	G,R,SK	**

NORTHWEST

The River Street Inn
100 Rivers Street West
Ketchum, ID 83340
(208) 726-3611

R,SA   *

Lewiston
Ramada Inn
621 21st Street
Lewiston, ID 83501
(208) 799-1000

A,G,H,R,S,NS   **

Pocatello
Comfort Inn
1333 Bench Rd.
Pocatello, ID 83201
(208) 237-8155

G,H,R,S   **

Holiday Inn
1399 Bench Road
Pocatello, ID 83201
(208) 237-1400

H,R,S,NS   *

Quality Inn
1555 Pocatello Creek Rd.
Pocatello, ID 83201
(208) 233-2200

G,H,R   **

Rexburg
Comfort Inn
SR 33
Rexburg, ID 83440
(208) 359-1311

G,H,R   *

Sandpoint
Quality Inn
807 N. 5th Ave.
Sandpoint, ID 83864
(208) 263-2111

G,R,S,SK   *

Twin Falls
Comfort Inn   G,H,R,S,SK   **
1893 Canyon Springs Rd.
Twin Falls, ID 83301
(208) 734-7494

MONTANA

Billings
Comfort Inn   H,R,S   *
2030 Overland Ave.
Billings, MT 59102
(406) 652-5200

Howard Johnson   A,H,R,NS   *
27th St. So.
Billings, MT 59101
(406) 248-4656

Quality Inn   G,H,R   *
2036 Overland Ave.
Billings, MT 59102
(406) 652-1320

Charlo
Allentown Motel & Restaurant   R   *
41000 US 93
Charlo, MT 59824
(406) 644-2588

East Glacier
East Glacier Motel   N/A   *
P.O. Box 93
East Glacier Park, MT 59434
(406) 226-5593

Glendive
Jordan Inn   R,S,NS   **
223 N. Merrill, Box 741
Glendive, MT 59330
(406) 365-5655; (800) 824-5067

NORTHWEST

Kings Inn   R,S,NS   *
1903 N. Merrill, Box 296
Glendive, MT 59330
(406) 365-5636

Great Falls
Comfort Inn   G,H,R,S   *
1120 9th St. S.
Great Falls, MT 59405
(406) 454-2727

Helena
Comfort Inn   G,H,R,S,T,SK   **
750 Fee St.
Helena, MT 59623
(406) 443-1000

Livingston
Budget Host Parkway Motel   NS,R,S,SK   **
1124 W. Park
Livingston, MT 59047
(406) 222-3840

Miles City
Friendship Inn   G,R,T   **
501 Main St.
Miles City, MT 59301
(406) 232-2450

Missoula
Inn at Broadway   G,H,R,T,SK   *
1609 W. Broadway
Missoula, MT 59802
(406) 543-7231

St. Ignatius
Sunset Motel   NS   *
32670 US 93
St. Ignatius, MT 59865
(406) 745-3900

NORTHWEST

Superior
Budget Host Big Sky Motel   G,NS,R,T   *
103 4th Ave E, Box 458
Superior, MT 59872
(406) 822-4831

Whitefish
Quality Inn   G,H,R,S,SK   **
920 Spokane Ave.
Whitefish, MT 59937
(406) 862-7600

OREGON

Albany
Comfort Inn   G,H,R,SA   **
251 Airport Rd.
Albany, OR 97321
(503) 928-0921

Baker City
Friendship Inn   G,R,T   *
810 Campbell St.
Baker City, OR 97814
(541) 523-2242

Bend
Comfort Inn   G,R,S,SA,SK   **
61200 S. US 97
Bend, OR 97702
(503) 388-2227

Cottage Grove
Comfort Inn   G,H,R   **
845 Gateway Blvd.
Cottage Grove, OR 97424
(503) 942-9747

Holiday Inn   G,H,R   *
1601 Gateway Blvd.
Cottage Grove, OR 97424
(503) 942-1000

Hillsboro
Marriott Residence Inn   N/A   ***
18855 NW Tanasbourne Dr.
Hillsboro, OR 97124
(503) 531-3200

Lake Oswego
Marriott Residence Inn   N/A   ***
15200 SW Bangy Rd.
Lake Oswego, OR 97035
(503) 684-2603

Medford
Oregon Lodge   A,H,NS   *
525 So. River Side
Medford, OR 97501
(541) 772-6133

Ontario
Holiday Inn   H,R,S,NS   *
1249 Tapadera Avenue
Ontario, OR 97914
(541) 889-8621

Pendleton
Vagabond Inn   R   *
201 S.W. Court Ave.
Pendleton, OR 97801
(541) 276-5253

Portland
Comfort Inn   G,R,S,T   **
431 NE Multnomah
Portland, OR 97232
(541) 233-7933

NORTHWEST

| Marriott Residence Inn
1710 NE Multnomah
Portland, OR 97232
(541) 288-0241 | N/A | *** |

| Vagabond Inn
518 N.E. Holladay St.
Portland, OR 97232
(541) 234-4391 | G,R,T | ** |

| Howard Johnson Hotel
7101 N.E. 82nd Avenue
Portland, OR 97220
(503) 255-6722 | A,R,S,NS | ** |

Roseburg

| Howard Johnson Lodge
978 N E Stephen
Roseburg, OR 97470
(503) 673-5082 | A,H,R,NS | * |

Springfield

| Rodeway Inn
3480 Hutton St.
Springfield, OR 97477
(503) 746-8471 | H,R,S | ** |

Camping Information Center
(503) 731-3411; (800) 452-5687

Oregon State Parks
(503) 378-6305

WASHINGTON

Bainbridge

| Bainbridge Inn
9200 Hemlock Ave. NE
Bainbridge, WA 98110
(206) 842-7564 | H | N/A |

Monarch Manor   SA   ***
7656 Yeomalt Pt. Dr. NE
Bainbridge Island, WA 98110
(206) 780-0112

Bellingham
Rodeway Inn   G,H,R,T   *
3710 Meridian St.
Bellingham, WA 98225
(206) 738-6000

Everett
Ramada Inn 4   A,G,R,S,NS   *
9602 19th Ave SE
Everett, WA 98208
(206) 337-9090

Kennewick
Comfort Inn   G,H,R,S   *
7801 W. Quinault Ave.
Kennewick, WA 99336
(509) 783-8396

Olympia
Holiday Inn   G,H,T   **
2300 Evergreen Park Dr.
Olympia, WA 98502
(206) 943-4000

Pullman
Quality Inn   G,H,R,T,SA   **
S.E. 1050 Bishop Blvd.
Pullman, WA 99163
(509) 332-0500

Richland
Vagabond Inn   G,R,T   *
515 George Washington Way
Richland, WA 99352
(509) 946-6117

Seattle

The Warwick Hotel   R,S,H   ***
401 Lenora St.
Seattle, WA 98121
(206) 443-4300

Howard Johnson   A,H,R,NS   *
20045 Intl Blvd, Pacific Hwy S
Seattle, WA 98198
(206) 878-3310

Marriott Residence Inn   A,S   ***
800 Fairview Avenue N.
Seattle, WA 98109
(206) 624-6000

Ramada Inn Northgate 1   A,G,H,R,S,T,NS   **
2140 N Northgate Way
Seattle, WA 98133
(206) 365-0700

Sequim

Econo Lodge   G,H,R,T, SK   *
801 E. Washington St.
Sequim, WA 98382
(206) 683-7113

Spokane

Comfort Inn   G,H,R,SA,SK   **
7111 N. Division
Spokane, WA 99208
(509) 467-7111

Rodeway Inn   G,R,T,SA   *
W. 827 1st Ave.
Spokane, WA 99204
(509) 838-8271

Ramada Inn Airport   G,H,R,NS   *
P.O. Box 19228
Spokane, WA 99219
(509) 838-5211

NORTHWEST

Spokane Bed & Breakfast   N/A   **
Reservation Service
E. 627 25th Ave.
Spokane, WA 99203
(509) 624-3776

Apple Tree Inn Motel   H,S,R,NS   **
N. 9508 Division
Spokane, WA 99203
(800) 323-5796

Cavanaugh's River Inn   H,S,R,NS   **
700 N. Division
Spokane, WA 99202
(800) THE-INNS

Tacoma
Ramada Inn Tacoma Dome   A,G,S,NS   **
Civic Center, 2611 East E Street
Tacoma, WA 98421
(206) 572-7272

Walla Walla
Comfort Inn   G,H,R,SA,SK   **
520 N. Second Ave.
Walla Walla, WA 99362
(509) 525-2522

White Salmon
Llama Ranch B&B   R   **
1980 Highway 141
White Salmon, WA 98672

Yakima
Bali Hai Motel   R,S,NS   **
710 N. 1st St.
Yakima, WA 98901
(509) 452-7178

Colonial Motor Inn   R,S,NS   **
1405 N. 1st St.
Yakima, WA 98901
(509) 453-8981

WYOMING

Buffalo
Econo Lodge   G,H,T,SK   *
333 Hart St.
Buffalo, WY 82834
(307) 684-2219

Crossroads Inn   H,R,S,NS   *
75 N. Bypass, PO Box 639
Buffalo, WY 82834
(307) 684-2256

Cheyenne
Comfort Inn   G,H,R   **
2245 Etchepare Dr.
Cheyenne, WY 82007
(307) 638-7202

Dubois
MacKenzie Highland Ranch   R   N/A
3945 Highway 26
Dubois, WY 82513
(307)-455-3415

Fossil Butte
Fossil Butte Motel   N/A   *
1424 Central Ave.
Kemmerer, WY 83101
(307) 877-3996

Lake V.N. Marina Motel   R   *
Hwy 233
Kemmerer, WY 83101
(307) 877-9669

Gillette
Ramada Limited   A,G,H,S,T,NS   *
608 E. 2nd Street
Gilette, WY 82716
(307) 682-9341

National 9 Inn   G,R,SA   *
1020 SR 51 E.
Gillette, WY 82716
(307) 682-5111

Lander
Budget Host Pronghorn Lodge   NS,R   **
150 E. Main St.
Lander, WY 82520
(307) 332-3940

Parkman
Foothills Ranch B&B   N/A   **
521 Pass Creek Rd.
Parkman, WY 82838
(307) 655-9362

Rock Springs
Rodeway Inn   G,R,T   *
1004 Dewar Dr.
Rock Springs, WY 82901
(307) 362-6673

South Yellowstone
Coachman Inn   N/A   *
112 Hwy 20
S. Yellowstone, WY
(307) 864-3141

Thermopolis
Cactus Inn Motel   N/A   *
605 S. 6th
Thermopolis, WY
(307) 864-3155

NORTHWEST

CANADA

Hotel Cost Codes (for average one-night stay)

*	$30-60/night
**	$61-100/night
***	$101-150/night
****	$151 and up/night
W	Hotel has weekly rates only

Note: costs may vary by season.

Hotel Amenity Codes

A	Airport nearby
H	Handicapped access
HS	Hair salon on premises
G	Golf within 10 miles
NS	Non-smoking rooms available
OB	Facility is on the beach
P	Playground on premises
R	Restaurant on premises
S	Swimming on premises
SA	Sauna on premises
SK	Skiing within 25 miles
T	Tennis within 10 miles

ALBERTA

Calgary

Ramada Hotel Downtown 708 8th Ave. SW Calgary, AB T2P 1H2 (403) 263-7600	G,R,S,HS,NS,SK	***
Budget Host Motor Inn 4420 16th Ave. NW Calgary, AB T3B 0M4 (403) 288-7115	N/A	**
Best Western 1947 18th Ave. NE Calgary, AB T2E 2T8 (403) 250-5015	N/A	**

Edmonton

Howard Johnson Plaza 10010 104 St. Edmonton, AB T5J OZ1	R,S	***
Travelodge 3414 118th Ave. Edmonton, AB T5W 0Z4 (403) 474-0456	G,NS,SK	*

Lethbridge

Travelodge Scenic Drive at 4th Ave. S. Lethbridge, AB T1J 0M8 (403) 327-2104	S,G,HS	*

Red Deer

Travelodge 2807 50 Ave. Red Deer, AB T4R 1H6 (403) 346-2011	G,NS,R,S,SK	**

CANADA

BRITISH COLUMBIA

Heffley Creek
Hitch & Rail   R   **
P.O. Box 115
Heffley Creek, BC VOE 1ZO
(604) 578-7112

Kamloops
Travelodge   G,NS,R,S,SA,SK,T   **
430 Columbia St.
Kamloops, BC V2C 2T5
(604) 372-8202

Nanaimo/Vancouver Island
Travelodge   G,SA   **
96 Terminal Ave. North
Nanaimo, BC V9S 4K8
(604) 754-6355

Pinantan Lake
Jandana Ranch   R   ***
Pinantan Lake, BC VOE 3EO
(604) 573-5800

Revelstoke
Travelodge   S,SK,T   **
1001 W 2nd St.
Revelstoke, BC VOE 2S0
(604) 837-2116

Vancouver
Westin Bayshore   R   ****
1601 W. Georgia St.
Vancouver, BC V6G 2V4
(604) 682-3377

The Four Seasons   R   ****
Vancouver, BC V6G 2V4
(602) 689-9333

Vernon
Travelodge	G,NS,SK	*
3000 28th Ave.		
Vernon, BC V1T 1W1		
(604) 545-2161		

Victoria
Regal Empress Hotel	R	****
721 Government St.		
Victoria, BC V8W 1WS		
(800) 828-7447		

Hotel Douglas	R	****
Victoria, BC V8W 1WS		
(602) 383-4157		

MANITOBA

Winnipeg
Travelodge Hotel	A,NS,R,S	**
360 Colony St.		
Winnipeg, Man. R3B 2P3		
(204) 786-7011		

NEW BRUNSWICK

Campbellton
Howard Johnson Hotel	H,NS,R	**
157 Water Street		
Campbellton, NB E3N 3H2		
(506) 753-4133		

Edmundston
Howard Johnson Plaza-Hotel	NS,R,S	**
100 Rice Street		
Edmundston, NB E3V 1T4		
(506) 739-7321		

Moncton
Holiday Inn Express   NS,H,R,S,G,SA   **
Box 5005
Trans-Canada Highway @ Magnetic Hill
Moncton, NB E1C 8R7
(506) 384-1050

Saint John
Howard Johnson Hotel   NS,H,R,S,G   **
400 Main Street @ Chesley Drive
Saint John, NB E2K 4N5
(506) 642-2622

NOVA SCOTIA

Halifax
Travelodge   N/A   **
374 Bedford Highway
Halifax, NS B3M 2C1
(902) 443-1576

ONTARIO

Aurora
Howard Johnson Hotel   NS,H,R   **
15520 Yonge St.
Aurora, ON L4G 1P2
(905) 727-1312

Belleville
Ramada Inn   G,H,R,S,T,NS   **
11 Bay Bridge Rd.
Belleville, ON K8N 4Z1
(613) 968-3411

Brantford
Travelodge Hotel   R,S   **
664 Colborne St.
Brantford, ON N3S 3P8
(519) 753-7371

Cornwall
Ramada Inn   G,H,R,S,T,NS,SA,SK   *
805 Brookdale Ave
Cornwall, ON K6J 4P3
(613) 933-8000

Hamilton
Howard Johnson Plaza-Hotel   H,R,S,NS,SA,SK   **
112 King St. E.
Hamilton, ON L8N 1A8
(905) 546-8111

Ramada Hotel   H,R,S,NS,SA,SK   **
150 King St. E.
Hamilton, ON L8N 1B2
(905) 528-3451

Kingston
Howard Johnson Hotel   A,G,H,R,S,T,NS   **
237 Ontario St.
Kingston, ON K7L 2Z4
(613) 549-6300

Kenora
Travelodge   G,R,S,SK,T   **
800 Sunset Strip
Kenora, ON P9N 1N9
(807) 468-3155

London
Ramada Inn 401   A,G,H,R,S,NS,SA   **
817 Exeter Road
London, ON N6E 1W1
(519) 681-4900

Markham
Howard Johnson Hotel   A,H,R,NS   **
555 Cochrane Dr.
Markham, ON L3R 8E3
(905) 479-5000

CANADA

Mississauga
Howard Johnson   A,R,NS   *
2420 Surveyor Road
Mississauga, ON L5N 4E6
(905) 858-8600

Morrisburg
Howard Johnson Hotel   G,R,S,T,NS,SA   **
Highway 2, P.O. Box 1140
Morrisburg, ON K0C 1X0
(613) 543-3788

Niagara Falls
Ramada Coral Inn   G,H,R,S,NS,SA   *
7429 Lundy's Lane
Niagara Falls, ON L2H 1G9
(905) 356-6116

North Bay
Travelodge   NS,S   **
1525 Seymour St.
North Bay, ON P1B 8J8
(705) 495-1133

Ottawa
Howard Johnson Plaza - Hotel   A,R,NS   **
140 Slater St.
Ottawa, ON K1P 5H6
(613) 238-2888

Ramada Hotel & Suites   H,R,NS   **
111 Cooper Street
Ottawa, ON K2P 2E3
(613) 238-1331

Peterborough
Peterborough Inn   G,H,R,S,NS,SA,SK   **
100 Charlotte Street
Peterborough, ON K9J 7L4
(705) 743-7272

Sault St. Marie
Ramada Inn / Conv. Ctr   G,H,R,S,NS,SA,SK   **
229 Great Northern Rd
Sault St. Marie, ON P6B 4Z2
(705) 942-2500

St. Catharines
Howard Johnson Hotel   G,H,R,S,NS,SA   **
89 Meadowvale Drive
St. Catharines, ON L2N 3Z8
(905) 934-5400

Sudbury
Ramada Inn-City Cntr   H,R,S,NS,SA,SK   **
85 Ste. Anne Road
Sudbury, ON P3E 4S4
(705) 675-1123

Toronto
Four Points Hotel   A,H,R,S,NS,SA   ***
5444 Dixie Rd
Toronto, ON L4W 2L2
(905) 624-1144

Colony Hotel   H,NS,R,S   **
City Hall
89 Chestnut Street
Toronto, ON M5G 1R1
(416) 977-0707

Howard Johnson Plaza - Hotel   A,H,R,S,NS,SA   **
2737 Keele St.
Toronto, ON M3M 2E9
(416) 636-4656

Windsor   G,H,NS,R   **
Ramada Inn Windsor
480 Riverside Drive West
Windsor, ON N9A 5K6
(519) 253-4411

CANADA

PRINCE EDWARD ISLAND

Charlottetown
Thriftlodge   G,NS,R,S   **
Highway 1
Charlottetown, PEI C1A 7L3
(902) 892-2481

QUEBEC

Charlemagne
Travelodge   G,R,T   **
115 Rue Chopin, Suite 106
Charlemagne, Que J52 4P8
(514) 582-5933

Montreal
Howard Johnson Hotel Plaza   A,R,NS,SA   ***
475 Rue Sherbrooke Ouest
Montreal, Que H3A 2L9
(514) 842-3961

Thriftlodge   R   *
1600 St. Hubert
Montreal, Que H2L 3Z3
(514) 894-3214

SASKATCHEWAN

Regina
Ramada Hotel Downtown   A,G,H,R,S,T,NS   ***
1919 Saskatchewan Drive
Regina, Sask. S4P 4H2
(306) 525-5255

Travelodge   G,NS,R,S   *
1110 Victoria Ave. East
Regina, Sask. S4N 7A9
(306) 565-0455

Pet-Friendly Resource Guide

This list of resources has been put together for any
additional needs that pet owners might have which weren't
addressed in the body of the text. These include:

- **Pet Travel Publications**
- **Pet Related Services and Clubs**
- **State Tourist Bureaus**

Pet Travel Publications

Take Your Pet Too! Fun Things to Do! ($16.95 + 3.00 S&H)
This publication covers the entire U.S. and Canada and includes advice, travel tips, new(!) nutritional information, pet-friendly concerts, museums, black-tie affairs, lobster dinners, etc. A few hotels, motels, and B&B's are included. It is currently the most unique guide on the market.
(See order form in the back)
MCE
P.O. Box 84
Chester, NJ 07930
(908) 879-7564

The Dogs' Guide To New York City ($14.95 + S&H)
This wonderful guide lists dog friendly department stores such as F.A.O. Schwarz, Bloomingdales, etc. There are several dog friendly restaurants listed as well. Dog clothiers, bookstores and hotels are listed.
Jack's City Dog Publcations
Richmond Press
(800) 560-1560

DogGone Newsletter ($24.00 for 6 Issues- 1 year)
A bimonthly publication with ideas, recipes, interesting outings and advice about all aspects of pet travel, DogGone is worth looking into.
DogGone
P.O. Box 651155
Vero Beach, FL 32965

On The Road Again With MAN'S BEST FRIEND ($14.95 for each section (e.g. New England)
A very entertaining guide, it describes in great detail all of the amenities of each featured hotel or inn. Worth getting for specific details about places to stay with your pet.
Dawbert Press
P.O. Box 2758
Duxbury, MA 02331
(800) 93-DAWBERT

Vacationing With Your Pet : Eileen's Directory of Pet Friendly Lodging ($19.95)

Many hotels, motels, and B&B's are found in this guide. Eileen also has valuable phone numbers, pet safety tips, and discussions of non-travel subjects. A valuable resource. She's also got "Doin' California With Your Pooch", a great hiking guide.

Pet-Friendly Publications
P.O. Box 8459
Scottsdale, AZ 85252
(800) 496-2665

Pets-R-Permitted: Hotel, Motel, Kennel & Petsitter ($12.95)

This guide has campgrounds as well as hotels and motels. Also listed are pet resorts, a unique inclusion in these guidebooks, as well as a helpful zipcode guide to accomodations near the town in which you wish to stay.

Purchase Registration
P.O. Box 11374
Torrance, CA 90510
(310) 374-6246

Take Your Pet USA ($11.95)

In its sixth printing, this guide lists hotels, motels, and special amenities for pets like exercise areas. It is a pocket guide with some coupons for travel.

Artco
12 Channel St.
Boston, MA 02210
(800) 255-8038

California Dog Lovers' Companion

This helpful guide to hotels and motels in California lists two dozen hotels in the San Diego area alone. This book includes many unexpected places to stay. The manager of the San Diego Princess, for example, has a very common sense attitude about pets and allows them in his wonderful resort. Worth getting.

(213) 730-5323

Pet-Related Services and Clubs

Pet Travel Consultant
Katrina Weiner
(916) 536-9859; (800) 205-0406
Trip packages are $25/city or $75/trip.
Includes maps and hotels.

Pet Care Savings Club
4501 Forbes Blvd.
Lanham, MD 20706
(800) 388-6978; (800) 388-7387
For $49.95 a year you receive 50% off all your pet friendly hotels.
You also get a hotel directory ,a 24-hour hotline for pet health and
behavior, "ANIMALOCATOR" tags for your furry friend, and
benefits which could save you up to $350 a year (in pet care products,
car rentals,etc.) And you can cancel anytime.

Hugs & Kisses Newsletter
2633 Lincoln Blvd. Suite 230
Santa Monica, CA 90405
(800) 430-4847
A quarterly newsletter with a wealth of excellent information on
training, feeding and caring for your pets by the world-renowned
expert, Warren Eckstein. Nobody knows your pet better. A big plus
is that this helps support the Hugs & Kisses Fund, a non-profit
organization dedicated to Warren's loving wife who devoted her life
to preventing animal suffering. This fund helps out all of the small,
hard-working organizations that have limited resources and do much
good work. Only $24.95/year. Write or call today.

Dog Square Dancing
Promenade Pups (Dallas County)
Woofing Hoofers (Simsbury, CT)
Create a club in your town!
Country Dance & Song Society (Music)
(413) 584-9913
United Square Dancers of America (Steps)
(205) 881-6044

Dog Lover's Dating Service
(For *you*, not your dog)
Dog Lover's Junction
P.O. Box 56
Highland, MD 20777-0056

Pet Training
David Dikeman's Command Performance
Dog Training System
(800) 237-1188

American Kennel Club
5580 Centerview Dr.
Raleigh, NC 27690-0643
Information   (919) 233-9767
Administration (212) 696-8200

Pet Sitters
Pet Sitters International
(800) 268-SITS

National Association of Professional Pet Sitters
(800) 296-7387

Kritter Sitters
Mar Vista, CA
(310) 398-8148

B&B for DOG
Denver, CO
(303) 745-8538

The Dog House
Doggie Day Care
(213) 549-WOOF

Woodbury
Motel & Apts.

407 Surf Ave.
N. Wildwood, NJ 08260
1½ Blocks To Beach

The Woodbury is _your_ place.
Your pet is our _Very Special Guest_.
10% off any stay at the Woodbury
if you mention that you read this special book.

State Tourist Bureaus

Alabama	(800) ALABAMA
Alaska	(800) 862-5275
Arizona	(888) 520-3444
Arkansas	(800) NATURAL
California	(800) TO-CALIF
Colorado	(800) COLORADO
Connecticut	(800) CT-BOUND
Delaware	(800) 441-8846
D. C.	(202) 789-7000
Florida	(904) 488-5607
Georgia	(800) VISIT-GA
Hawaii	(800) 353-5846
Idaho	(800) 635-7820
Illinois	(800) ABE-0121
Indiana	(800) 289-6646
Iowa	(800) 345-IOWA
Kansas	(800) 2-KANSAS
Kentucky	(800) 225-TRIP
Louisiana	(800) 33-GUMBO
Maine	(800) 533-9595
Maryland	(800) 543-1036
Massachussetts	(800) 447-MASS
Michigan	(800) 5432-YES
Minnesota	(800) 657-3700
Mississippi	(800) WARMEST
Missouri	(800) 877-1234
Montana	(800) VISIT-MT
Nebraska	(800) 228-4307
Nevada	(800) NEVADA-8
New Hampshire	(800) FUN-IN-NH
New Jersey	(800) JERSEY-7

State Tourist Bureaus (cont'd)

New Mexico   (800) 545-2040
New York   (800) CALL-NYS
North Carolina   (800) VISIT-NC
North Dakota   (800) 435-5663
Ohio   (800) BUCKEYE
Oklahoma   (800) 652-OKLA
Oregon   (800) 547-7842
Pennsylvania   (800) VISIT-PA
Rhode Island   (800) 556-2484
South Carolina   (800) 868-2492
South Dakota   (800) SDAKOTA
Tennessee   (800) 836-6200
Texas   (800) 88-88-TEX
Utah   (800) 200-1160
Vermont   (800) VERMONT
Virginia   (800) VISIT-VA
Washington   (800) 544-1800
West Virginia   (800) 225-5982
Wisconsin   (800) 372-2737
Wyoming   (800) 225-5996

WHEN WAS THE LAST TIME
YOU AND YOUR DOG SAVED A LIFE?

WHAT? A non-competitive dog walk-athon to raise money for the fight against human & animal cancers

FOR WHOM? The American Cancer Society with a portion of the net proceeds to be donated to the Animal Medical Center (Donaldson-Atwood Cancer Clinic)

CALL FOR REGISTRATION INFORMATION FOR A TAIL-WAGGING GOOD TIME

THE AMERICAN CANCER SOCIETY • 212/237-3872

Cypress Inn
Carmel-By-The-Sea, California

Doris Day welcomes you and your pet(s) to visit this historic property located within steps of all the shops, restaurants & galleries of Carmel-by-the-Sea!

CYPRESS INN

Lincoln & 7th Sts.

P. O. Box Y

Carmel, CA 93921

408/624-3871
800/443-7443

Fax: 408/624-8216

DOG W🐾SH

Dog Beach Dog Wash

Do-It-Yourself Grooming & Accessories

2 1/2 Blocks from Dog Beach, San Diego's
largest off-leash canine playground

4933 Voltaire St. • San Diego, CA 92107

(619) 523-1700 • www.dogwash.com/dogs

Offering San Diego's finest selection of floating toys, grooming
supplies, and gifts for dogs and those who love them

7 a.m. to 9 p.m., 7 days a week

Certified
Canine
Specialists

PIJAC

THE HILLTOP INN
Route 117, Sugar Hill, NH 03585
800-770-5695 / 603-823-5695
Fax 603-823-5518
Email mike.hern@hilltopinn.com

1895 Victorian nestled in the peaceful village of Sugar Hill in the heart of the White Mountains. A romantic escape offering large breakfasts, comfortable guest rooms, suites and a cottage all filled with antiques, handmade quilts and immaculate private baths. Relax on our porches or by a crackling fire. Stroll down quiet country roads with spectacular mountain views. We are 10 minutes from Franconia Notch. **Pets very welcomed.** AAA ◆◆◆ MC, VISA, DISCOVER
The Hilltop Inn has been featured in *Yankee, Outside, Country Victorian, Boston Globe* and numerous travel guides.

NJ Pets

Show this ad and receive
1 free pig ear or 2" fur mouse cat toy!
Limit one per ad.
Good one time only.

Give The Gift Of Fun: A Year Of DogGone!

[ ] Hey, I want my friends the discover fun places to go and do cool stuff with their dog! Enter a gift subscription for 1 year (6 issues of **DogGone**™) for just $24.00. (For gifts to Florida residents, add $1.44 state sales tax.)

Name _____

Address_____

City _____ State _____ Zip _____

Dog's Name(s) _____

Breed(s) _____

[ ] Gift Subscription from_____

Mail this coupon with check or M.O. payable to DogGone to:
DogGone, P.O. Box 651155, Vero Beach, FL 32965-1155.

Personalized Travel Information

AN EXCLUSIVE
SERVICE FOR
DOGGONE
SUBSCRIBERS

Name _____

Address_____

City _____ State _____ Zip _____

Telephone (_____) _____

I'd like information on _____ (city or state).

Additional city(ies) or state(s) _____

_____ (Enclose $10.00 each)

Accommodations Preference:

| | Bed & Breakfast/Inn | | Farm/Ranch | | Resort
| | Campground/RV Park | | Hotel/Motel | | All

Month/Date of Planned Trip_____

Mail coupon to P.O. Box 651155, Vero Beach, FL 32965-1155.
PHOTOCOPIES NOT ACCEPTED. ORIGINAL COUPON MUST BE MAILED.

Turtle Beach
₹ R E S O R T ★

a "KEY WEST" style waterfront inn

★ Each charming cottage w/private hot tub,
   patio & distinctive unique decor

★ Access to secluded Turtle Beach

★ Tropical, lush landscaping

★ Watersports, fishing & private dock

★ Free bicycles, fishing poles, & paddleboat

★ New bay front pool

★ Fine waterfront dining next door

★ Tropical, private bay front villas & studios

9049 Midnight Pass Rd. Siesta Key, FL 34242
(941) 349-4554 Fax: **(941) 918-0203**
Email: grubi@ix.netcom.com

ORDER FORM

MCE offers pet lovers **two** great guides for pet travel. These books make excellent gifts for pet-loving friends and family.

Take Your Pet Along - 1001 Places to Stay With Your Pet
A comprehensive guide to hotels, motels and inns that welcome you and your pet (U.S. & Canada). 280 pages, GBC-bound.

Take Your Pet Too! - Fun Things To Do
The ultimate pet-compatible vacation planner - includes resorts, beaches, parks, campgrounds, and fun events across the U.S.

MCE Pet Travel Book Order Form

Name: _____

Address: _____

City/State/Zip: _____

Payment: Check
(Check one)   Money Order
                  American Express (enter data below)

          Card Number: _____
          Exp. Date: _____

Quantity	Description	Unit Price	Total
	Take Your Pet Along	$14.95	
	Take Your Pet Too	$16.95	
	Both Books - SAVE 15%!	$26.95	
* Make checks payable to MCE		NJ Residents add 6% tax	
Send to:		Shipping & Handling	$3.00 (any order)
MCE P.O. Box 84 Chester, NJ 07930-0084		**TOTAL ENCLOSED**	

Notes